LEGAL SECRETARY'S DESK BOOK

--WITH FORMS

LEGAL SECRETARY'S DESK BOOK
--WITH FORMS

Betty Kennedy Thomae

Parker Publishing Company, Inc.

West Nyack, New York

Library of Congress Cataloging in Publication Data

Thomae, Betty Kennedy.
 Legal secretary's desk book--with forms.

 1. Legal secretaries--Handbooks, manuals, etc.
I. Title.
KF319.T45   651'.9'34   73-5788
ISBN 0-13-529321-9

TO

KENNETH P. BESSEY, ESQUIRE

Whose many years of patience and training
have helped to write this book.

Acknowledgments

A special thanks to John P. Bessey, Esquire, for his cooperation in supplying me with material for Chapters 1, 7, and 9.

My appreciation also goes to Dianne Brewer for helping me with the section on trial docket in Chapter 9, and many thanks to Marjorie Alexander, PLS of Santa Clara, California, for her contribution to Chapter 7.

Betty Kennedy Thomae, CPS, PLS

A Word from the Author
About the Scope and Value of the Book

This book provides a ready source of solutions to a large variety of problems in the law office. For instance, your attorney-boss may say "I need a guardian's account in the May Ross guardianship right away." Perhaps you have never prepared a guardian's account and need specific instructions. You will find in this book a special section on receiving and disbursing guardianship funds and how to prepare an account—just waiting for you in Chapter Six.

Your office may have a filing problem—how to handle specific types of cases, whether to use categorical filing, straight alphabetical or numerical. You will find a broad range of suggestions on filing in the law office, e.g., how to set up special files such as a simple will file, an estate plan file, an abstract continuation file, and many others.

Good management is a must in the law office, and you must constantly demonstrate that you have management ability and can run the administrative side of the office. In Chapter Four, you will find lots of proven, successful techniques on ways to manage the office, e.g., how to keep the supplies flowing smoothly, and how to manage your attorney's fees without supervision. You will also find out how to pay the bills and how to keep expensive equipment working smoothly.

Whether your office becomes involved in Probate Work, Domestic Relations, Trial Work or Tax Work, you will have at your fingertips an invaluable source of pointers, tips, and workable ways of handling day to day situations that arise in each of these areas.

Want to make yourself outstanding in your *total* performance? You'll find nine effective ways to do this in Chapter Three.

While you will find the Table of Contents helpful in guiding you to the subject matter of each chapter, be sure to use the handy index at the back of the book to pinpoint specific examples and subject areas you wish to locate quickly.

Betty Kennedy Thomae, CPS, PLS
Columbus, Ohio

Contents

Notary Public . Guidelines for making up a special form
book for legal pleadings and other documents, to save
dictation time . Tips on how to perform special duties
such as signing on bank accounts, making up a tickler file,
handling the lawyer's appointment calendar . Strategic
ways to handle your lawyer's incoming mail . Nine ways
to help your lawyer with his personal affairs . And yes,
even a section on housekeeping duties!

Seven successful ways to demonstrate to your lawyer that
you have management ability . Pointers on how to order
supplies for the law office . How to organize your work
load . How to supervise a junior secretary . How to
receive and bank your attorney's fees . How to pay your
lawyer's bills . And what to do about the office equipment . Tips on what attitude to take towards your co-
workers . And how the experienced secretary treats a
new associate or law clerk . How to set up a trust account
for clients' trust monies.

Alphabetical, numerical and subject files and how they can
be applied to the law office . How to set up an Estate
Plan File . How to set up a subject file for the lawyer's
reference materials . How to use a form file for legal
blanks . How to use a file to retain clients' abstracts .
How to set up a special file for abstract continuations so
that they can be located instantly . How to file supplements to Reference Materials and Tax Guides.

Takes you through the lawyer's entire probate practice,
including the simple will and codicil, trust wills, guardianships, administering estates and adoptions, with many,
many sample illustrations of pleadings and documents .

LEGAL SECRETARY'S DESK BOOK

--WITH FORMS

Developing a Clearer
Understanding of Law
and the Secretary's Role

As a legal secretary, you customarily concern yourself with local laws and customs. However, in order to acquire a knowledge of the background and derivation of our laws, it is well for you to have an insight into the various types of law in use in this country and in others. For example, the common law (or unwritten law) in use in this country today is essentially the common law of England.

A background in the structure of the law is not only enlightening and broadening, but necessary to the legal secretary. Included in this chapter is a brief digest of the types of law currently in use in the United States and Europe. After familiarizing yourself with the digest, you will have a clearer understanding of International Law, the Justinian Code, the Code Napoleon, the Federal Code, Common Law, Statutory Law, etc., and the important role each segment of the law plays in our society.

Following is an outline of the types of law that are in use today:

1. Common Law.
2. Statutory or Code Law.
3. Federal Law.
4. Code Napoleon.
5. Roman Law.
6. International Law.

Here is a brief description of the above categories:

COMMON LAW

Common law is that great body of so-called unwritten law, which is in use in the United States today and which originated in England. "Unwritten" refers to the fact that the laws have not been codified. It is law based upon general usage and custom.

There is no *national* common law, only that in use as adopted by the *various states.* All of the states, including the District of Columbia, have adopted common law, with the exception of Louisiana, which uses Civil Law.

STATUTORY OR CODE LAW

A statute is an act of a legislature. Sometimes a statute may incorporate common law, and some states codify their statutes, or put them in code form.

FEDERAL LAW

Our constitution vests the judicial power of the United States in the Supreme Court. Congress has the power to create inferior courts from time to time, and to establish special courts such as the Tax Court of the United States. Annually, the Chief Justice of the Supreme Court summons the chief judges of each circuit court to a Judicial Conference of the United States. This Conference studies conditions in the various districts.

The Supreme Court consists of a Chief Justice and eight associate justices, six of whom constitute a quorum. The justices of the Supreme Court are appointed by the President with the consent of the Senate, and they hold tenure-in-office, pending good behavior. The decisions of the United States Supreme Court are final.

Each session of the Supreme Court commences on the first Monday in October of each year.

CODE NAPOLEON[1]

[This code] was promulgated in 1804. When Napoleon became emperor, the name was changed to "Code Napoleon," by which it is

---

[1]Reprinted from Black's Law Dictionary, Fourth Edition, by permission of West Publishing Company.

still often designated, though it is now officially styled by its original name of "Code Civil." *[The Code Civil]* embodies the civil law of France.

ROMAN LAW[2]

[Roman Law], in a general sense, comprehends all the laws which prevailed among the Romans, without regard to the time of their origin, including the collections of Justinian.

In a more restricted sense, the Germans understand by this term merely the law of Justinian, as adopted by them.

In England and America, it appears to be customary to use the phrase, indifferently with "the civil law," to designate the whole system of Roman jurisprudence, including the *Corpus Juris Civilis;* or, if any distinction is drawn, the expression "civil law" denotes the system of jurisprudence obtaining in those countries of continental Europe which have derived their juridical notions and principles from the Justinian collection, while "Roman Law" is reserved as the proper appellation of the body of law developed under the government of Rome from the earliest times to the fall of the empire.

INTERNATIONAL LAW

International Law covers the dealings of nations with each other. Private International Law, dealing with the acts and rights of individuals in one nation within another nation, is a separate body of law.

International Law consists of two types—unwritten and conventional. The conventional law is derived from international agreements and treaties. The unwritten law, like common law, is partly based on custom and usage. Attempts have been made from time to time to codify International Law.

An international organization that deals with international problems is the United Nations. The charter was adopted June 26, 1945, in San Francisco. The United Nations may file a suit against a nation.

If you would like to make a complete study of the types of law listed above, except Code Napoleon and Roman Law, see *American Jurisprudence.* Most law libraries have this set.

Ibid.

The Lawyer-Client Relationship

The lawyer's relationship with his client involves such things as professional ethics and privileged communications.

ETHICS

In the matter of ethics, the lawyer is usually guided by standards adopted by his local, state, or national Bar Association. The canons of the American Bar Association [3] are as follows:

Canon 1: A lawyer should assist in maintaining the integrity and competence of the legal profession.

Canon 2: A lawyer should assist the legal profession in fulfilling its duty to make legal counsel available.

Canon 3: A lawyer should assist in preventing the unauthorized practice of law.

Canon 4: A lawyer should preserve the confidences and secrets of a client.

Canon 5: A lawyer should exercise independent professional judgment on behalf of a client.

Canon 6: A lawyer should represent a client competently.

Canon 7: A lawyer should represent a client zealously within the bounds of the law.

Canon 8: A lawyer should assist in improving the legal system.

Canon 9: A lawyer should avoid even the appearance of professional impropriety.

For a complete reprinting of the canons, the ethical considerations, and the disciplines of the American Bar Association as applicable to member lawyers, write The American Bar Association, 1155 E. 60th Street, Chicago, Illinois 60637. Your lawyer is very likely a member of the American Bar Association, and it would be time well spent for you to read the entire reprint to familiarize yourself with the standards of professional conduct.

---

[3]Taken from the American Bar Association's Formal Ethics Opinion 316.

PRIVILEGED COMMUNICATION

Privileged communication involves the attorney's immunity as to his client's confidences while on the witness stand. The mere fact that he is an attorney at law does not generally make him an incompetent witness, but he is limited in what he must disclose of his client's affairs on the witness stand in a suit for or against his client.

The rule covering the attorney's limitation in disclosure is a long-established rule of common law. Under this policy, even if the attorney is willing to disclose information about his client without his client's consent, he may not do so.

If you are interested in a thorough study of Privileged Communications, consult *American Jurisprudence,* Volume 58, pages 259 through 595.

CLIENT'S CONFIDENCE IN THE SECRETARY

The client's relationship with you influences his relationship with the attorney. It is important that the client have confidence in you and in your ability not to divulge confidential information, which is often imparted to you through dictation and typing. Also, the client must be assured that you will efficiently and accurately perform your portion of the work to be done. If the client has no confidence in you, his or her confidence in the attorney will not be as great; for the client would expect the attorney to hire competent, trustworthy employees.

The lawyer's standard of ethics also pertain to you. Many clients will "pour out" their troubles to you, and you should remember at all times that these communications are confidential and should not be repeated outside the office.

GREETING THE CLIENTS

You should keep your calendar in conformance with the attorney's so that you will be aware of each appointment. When the receptionist informs the lawyer that his client has arrived, the lawyer may wish you to accompany the client into his office. You should greet the client by name, take his or her coat and precede the client into the attorney's office. If the client is a new one whom the attorney has not met, you may say "Mr. Black, this is Mrs. Jones.

She has had a death in the family" (your having obtained this information at the time of making the appointment by telephone). You should then leave the office, closing the door behind you. When the client leaves, you should have his or her coat ready.

TELEPHONE RELATIONSHIP WITH CLIENTS

Many clients will depend on you to relay their problems to the attorney; they often feel that in doing so they are not taking up so much of the attorney's valuable time. You should, in these cases, be careful not to offer "advice," lest you be guilty of "unauthorized practice of law." Often, the clients will feel that you know as much about law as the lawyer. In such cases, you should be firm in making it clear to the client that you are not permitted to "give advice."

Making appointments with the client over the telephone is discussed in greater detail in Chapter Three.

TWO

How to Use
the Law Library

In the smaller law office, you may be in charge of the law library; whereas the larger law library may be in the charge of a law clerk or even a librarian. In any case, it is well for you to have a basic concept of what is in the law library, how it might be arranged, and how it is used. This chapter will attempt to look briefly into these points.

Outline of Basic Legal Material

1. STATUTES

(a) **Federal.** The laws enacted by Congress are first published officially as "slip laws," that is, each law in a separate leaflet. Some time after the end of each session of Congress they are reprinted in a bound volume of the *Statutes at Large.* They are published unofficially in *United States Code Congressional and Administrative News.* This publication is first issued in semi-monthly pamphlets and later in bound volumes.

The *Statutes at Large* have been codified, that is, arranged by subject matter and given title numbers in the *United States Code.* Two unofficial editions of the U.S.C. exist—the *U.S. Code Annotated* and the *Federal Code Annotated.* The annotations cite court and administrative opinions that have interpreted each section. In addition, the annotations offer considerable historical data and occasional editorial comment.

(b) State. The laws enacted by a State legislature are published as "Session Laws." This is the most common title, but it is not universal. Whatever the title, the distinguishing feature is that the laws are published in the order of their passage, without any regard to subject matter. Usually, there is some advance form of publication similar to the "slip laws" of Congress. These, in turn, are codified into "Codes," similar to the U.S.C., though they may be called "Revisions," "Compilations," etc. Just as in the case of the U.S.C., codes are compilations of the laws in force, arranged by subject matter. Thus, for instance, all of the laws relating to labor, which have been enacted through the years and originally published in different volumes of the Session Laws, are collected into one title of the Code.

The Codes are the most frequently used form of the law, but the Session Laws must be available for research and reference. In most states there is also an annotated edition of the code. Although this edition is published commercially, it is, for all practical purposes, treated as the official code.

2. TREATIES

Prior to 1950, treaties and international agreements (with some variations) were published in the *Statutes at Large*. Beginning in 1950, treaties and agreements have been published in a separate series of volumes called *United States Treaties and Other International Agreements*, cited as U.S.T. The treaties are also published in slip form; they may be ordered individually or a subscription may be entered for the series (cited as T.I.A.S.). A most useful reference guide to the treaties is an annual pamphlet called "Treaties in Force."

3. REPORTS

(a) Federal. The highest federal court is, of course, the Supreme Court of the United States. The opinions of this Court are published officially in the *United States Reports* and unofficially in *Lawyers' Edition* and *Supreme Court Reporter* (since 1882). The unofficial editions carry editorial comment. Supreme Court opinions are available in slip form and in advance-sheet form. Probably the quickest reporting is in the *United States Law Week* or the *CCH, U.S. Supreme Court Bulletin*.

The intermediate federal court is the U.S. Court of Appeals. Each circuit, of which there are ten, and the District of Columbia, has a Court of Appeals. The opinions of these courts are reported in the *Federal Reporter*. Each volume of this Reporter has a map showing the states embraced in each circuit.

The lowest federal court is the District Court. Each state has at least one District Court; the more populous states have two or more. The opinions of these courts have been reported in *Federal Supplement* since 1931. Prior to that date, they were reported in *Federal Reporter*. Not all of the opinions of the district courts are reported, however. Often, opinions that appear in the *Federal Rules Decisions* will not appear in *Federal Supplement*. The same is true of specialized loose-leaf services on such topics as taxation, trade regulation, administrative law, etc.

There are a number of special federal courts, the decisions of which are reported "officially" in their own series of reports and also in *Federal Reporter* or *Federal Supplement*. These are Courts of Claims, Courts of Custom and Patent Appeals and Customs Courts. The Court of Military Appeals and the Tax Court are reported only in their own official reports or, in the case of the Tax Court, in the loose-leaf tax services.

(b) State. Each state has its own judicial system, usually comprised of the same three levels found in the federal system. The titles of these courts will differ from state to state. For example, "supreme" does not always mean the highest court of the state; in fact, the Supreme Court in New York is a court of original jurisdiction, the intermediate court is the Appellate Division and the highest court is the Court of Appeals.

Many states publish the decisions of their courts in an official series of reports, and the courts prefer that these be cited in briefs. A library should at least have available the official reports of its own state, if not those of other states.

State court decisions are reported unofficially in *The National Reporter System,* published by West Publishing Company. This series groups the states into regions: Atlantic, Northeastern, Northwestern, Pacific, Southeastern, Southwestern and Southern, plus two special reporters, *New York Supplement* and *California Reporter*. With the exception of New York and California, the National Reporters generally report only the decisions of the highest state courts. Most private libraries rely on the regional reporters for decisions of state courts other than those in their own states.

(c) **Annotated Reports.** Selected cases, both federal and state, are also reported in *American Law Reports Annotated* (cited as A.L.R.). These are published by the Lawyers Cooperative Publishing Company, and are tied in with their other publications, the *Lawyer's Edition* of the Supreme Court Reports and *American Jurisprudence.* The cases are reported with extensive editorial comment, sometimes equivalent to a brief or a memorandum of law. This set runs from 1918 to date. A special digest, with supplementary volumes of case finders, cross references, added annotations, etc., is necessary for access to the reports.

4. ADMINISTRATIVE AGENCIES

Many federal and some state administrative agencies publish their decisions and rulings. In some cases, their regulations are also published.

5. DIGESTS

Digests provide a method of getting into the reported court decisions by subject. The most comprehensive digest is published by West Publishing Co., which uses the same key-numbered headnotes that are used in their other reports. This digest, the *American Digest System,* digests all reported cases from 1658 to date. This is divided into units, starting with the *Century Digest* (1658-1896) and running through six Decennial digests up to 1956. The *General Digest* volumes, published annually, keep the set current.

The *American Digest System* is so bulky, both to house and to use, that many libraries also keep limited digests on hand for purposes of convenience. The *Federal Digest* and *Modern Federal Practice Digest* cover all federal court decisions. The *United States Supreme Court Digest* covers only Supreme Court decisions. In addition, there are digests for each of the regional reporters of the *National Reporter System*—such as Atlantic, Pacific, etc. All of these are published by West Publishing Company and use the same key-number system. The Lawyers Cooperative Publishing Co. also publishes a *Digest of the United States Supreme Court Reports,* using the index system of A.L.R., L.Ed., and Am.Jur.

Digests for individual states are published, mainly by West Publishing Company but occasionally by other publishers, and any library should certainly have the digest for its home state.

6. SHEPARD'S CITATIONS

These familiar, red books are an essential legal tool—so essential, that "Shepardize" has become an accepted verb in legal terminology. There is a *Shepard's* for each state and for each unit of the *National Reporter System,* including Federal and United States reports. There is much information to be gleaned from Shepard's, too much to be discussed here. However, the publisher can supply a useful pamphlet on "How to use Shepard's Citations," and each unit has an explanatory preface.

Basically, *Shepard's* gives the "history" of a case, that is, whether it has been affirmed or reversed by a higher court. It also indicates where the case has been cited in other court opinions and in selected law reviews, and whether it has been followed, distinguished, etc. Cross references to pertinent official or unofficial reports are also given. The same type of information is given for statutes—whether they have been amended or repealed and where they are cited in opinions. Citations are also given to recent law review articles and notes.

A number of the older federal administrative agencies are included in *Shepard's U.S. and Federal Citations,* but not all. Rather recently, Shepard's published the *Federal Labor Law Citations,* and there has been some talk about expanding their coverage of administrative agencies.

The library should have the appropriate *Shepard's* for every set of reports that it holds.

7. LEGAL ENCYCLOPEDIAS

The two current encyclopedias are *Corpus Juris Secundum* and *American Jurisprudence 2d* (still incomplete). In effect, encyclopedias amount to thumbnail treatises on legal topics. They are supplemented annually, and are a good starting point for research—particularly if the topic is one on which the library does not have a definitive treatise.

There are also a few "encyclopedias" for individual states, which are confined to the law as interpreted by the courts of the respective states.

8. TREATISES

There are thousands of treatises, or textbooks, on specific legal topics. Some, such as *Williston on Contracts, Wigmore on Evidence* and *Fletcher on Corporations,* are considered classics. Others make a name for themselves as time goes on.

Some treatises are general in nature and others are restricted to a particular state practice. Whatever the case, these are considered a "secondary source" of law in that the courts are not bound by their statements. Nevertheless, they are cited and are a useful starting point for research.

9. RESTATEMENTS OF THE LAW

The American Law Institute has, for about thirty years, been engaged in compiling the *Restatements.* Because this has been compiled by outstanding authorities on each topic, it is often cited with approval by the courts.

10. PERIODICALS

Legal periodicals, particularly those published by law schools and professional associations, are another "secondary" source. These are best approached through the *Index to Legal Periodicals.* The *Business Law Articles* (loose leaf) is also useful, particularly for periodicals not held by the library. The *Index to Foreign Legal Periodicals* was started in 1960 as a quarterly with annual cumulations.

11. LEGAL DICTIONARIES

The need for law dictionaries is obvious. *Black's* and *Ballentine's* are the most common. *Words and Phrases,* in 73 volumes and supplemented annually, attempts to give every definition appearing in court decisions.

12. SUBJECT BIBLIOGRAPHIES

Frequently, a bibliography on a certain subject is prepared by a bar association library or by some other librarian and published in a periodical, which is indexed in the I.L.P. If such a bibliography turns up on a pertinent subject, much research time can be saved.

Arrangement

Most private law libraries arrange their collections by jurisdiction, with some deviation towards classification for subjects, such as taxation, that have a voluminous amount of material. In any case, reference sources such as digests, codes, encyclopedias and treatises should be placed on tables, where they can be consulted in comfort. Reports, session laws and statutes may be shelved in the stacks.

It is most logical to house the federal materials in one area. Included would be the *United States Reports* (official and unofficial) the *Federal* and *Federal Supplement Reports,* the *Federal Rules Decisions and Service,* the *Federal and Supreme Court Digests,* the *U.S. Code* and *Statutes at Large.* The *Code of Federal Regulation* and the *Federal Register* could be in this section or, if there is a large collection of administrative law material, these two sets could be shelved in an administrative-law section.

Home-state and municipal codes, reports, digests and regulations would naturally be housed in one area. Any material for other states should be adjacent to the home-state section.

Shepard's Citations is generally shelved with the appropriate reporter or code. The system of shelving them all together, arranged alphabetically, is preferred by some libraries, but the chance of misshelving is greater with this plan.

Directories, which include the law lists, Who's Who, business and association guides and any financial reference books, such as *Moody's* or *Standard and Poor,* should be grouped together.

Periodicals should be grouped together and shelved alphabetically.

The *National Reporter System* may be shelved in stacks, but the *American Digest Series* should be arranged on work tables.

Treatises are usually shelved in the main reading room and arranged by author. A few private libraries attempt to group treatises by subject, but this requires some rather arbitrary decisions in cases where subjects overlap. Unless the entire library is to be classified, which would mean that loose-leaf services would be shelved within the subject sections of the treatises, it seems unwise to try to classify *only* the treatises.

The entire subject of classified arrangement is a thorny one. Most libraries will find that, for purposes of convenience, certain subject areas require classification. Taxation is one of these areas. The loose-leaf services on federal taxation should certainly be near the Tax Court reports and the Cumulative Bulletins. Having gone this far, it seems feasible to add the tax treatises and the tax periodicals. Loose-leaf services for state taxes could be in the tax section or in the state section, but experience shows that tax lawyers make more use of the state-law service than do general-practice lawyers.

Labor law is another example. The loose-leaf services on labor are more conveniently shelved with the N.L.R.B. decisions than in the general-services section. The same is true of treatises and periodicals on labor laws.

Cataloging

The small library does not usually require cataloging, but it might be necessary in the larger libraries. Catalog cards may be ordered from the Library of Congress. A complete study of the subject of cataloging may be found in *Manual of Procedures for Private Law Libraries,* Rothman, 1966, published for the American Association of Law Libraries.

You may be called upon to locate a book or return one to the shelves. Or, the up-and-coming position of legal assistant or paralegal technician may eventually involve legal research. For a complete study of how to go about legal research, see *Fundamentals of Legal Research* by Ervin H. Pollack, published by the Foundation Press, Inc., a subsidiary of West Publishing Company.

Modern Secretarial Procedures
in the Law Office

Certain duties can only be classified under the broad term of secretarial procedures. This chapter will cover some of these duties, such as signing on a bank account, handling the mail, tickler systems, the appointment calendar, acting as a witness, acting as a notary public, making up a form book of pre-dictated forms, being a personal secretary and, yes, even housekeeping duties. Following is a brief insight into each of these classifications.

When You Are a Signer on a Bank Account

Often, office procedures can be facilitated when you sign the checks; it saves the attorney's valuable time for more important matters. After you have made the necessary arrangements with your boss and at the bank, proceed to sign all checks with the signature as given to the bank. Signing checks is a position of trust, and it should not be taken lightly. Each disbursement should be verified before it is made. Determine the availability of funds by keeping a careful running bank balance in the checkbook, and be careful not to disburse funds that are not there; in other words, do not overdraw the account. Make deposits regularly and keep a careful record of them, and balance the checkbook once a month with the bank statement. Canceled checks are best preserved in numerical order in a check-size file cabinet.

If you sign on more than one account, e.g., a trust account, an office account, and a personal checking account for your lawyer, exercise great care to see that the funds go into the proper account and disbursements are made from the appropriate account.

Handling the Incoming Mail

When you open the daily mail, do more than slit the envelopes and hand the mail to the attorney. Annotate, answer routine correspondence, and weed out unwanted advertising that you are certain the attorney has no interest in.

Upon opening the mail, save only those envelopes that show a return address that is not on the letter, and attach it to the letter. The mail may then be separated into groups, for example:

1. Mail that requires action to be taken by the attorney.
2. Mail that requires no action and that may be placed in the file box (after ascertaining the attorney's preference as to whether he does or does not wish to see this type of mail).
3. Letters that are routine and may be answered by you, either over the attorney's signature or over your own.
4. Requests for charitable donations.
5. Invoices, either business or personal.
6. Advertisements.
7. Checks for office fees or costs.

Group #1: If a piece of mail requires action to be taken by the attorney, there are several things you can do to expedite the attorney's handling of this mail. First, if it refers to previous correspondence, pull out the file jacket and give it to the attorney along with the letter. If he wishes to refer to previous correspondence before dictating a reply, he will have the necessary material in front of him.

Second, annotate the letter. Make a brief notation in the margin as to previous action, underline key sentences and anything that you think might refresh his memory quickly and save time.

Third, if the letter refers to a calendar date for an event, mark the attorney's calendar and note on the letter that you have done so.

Group #2: If the attorney does not wish to see this type of mail, place it directly in the file box for later placement in the appropriate folder.

Group #3: There are always certain types of letters tha refer to routine matters, and that may be handled by you, either over the attorney's signature, or your own. In either case, bear in mind at all times the policy of the attorney or his firm and remember that you have that image to project, not your own personality. Also, be guided by the lawyer's professional code of ethics, as discussed in Chapter One. Following are three examples of the type of letter you might write.

FIGURE 3-1

**Sample Letter Written Routinely by You
Over the Attorney's Signature**

BLACK & JONES
Attorneys at Law
30 Main Street
Anytown, U.S.A.

Harold H. Black
Gerald M. Jones

August 1, 19

Mr. and Mrs. Carl Rinehart
100 E. Town Street
Columbus, Ohio 43215

In re Mary M. Connors
36 E. 19th Avenue
Columbus, Ohio

Dear Mr. and Mrs. Rinehart:

Your Christmas card addressed to Mrs. Mary M. Connors was forwarded to me as Executor of Mrs. Connors' estate.

I regret to inform you that Mrs. Connors died last December 5.

Very truly yours,

BLACK & JONES

Harold H. Black

HHB:rjk

FIGURE 3-2

Sample Letter Written Routinely by You
Discharging Bondsman for a Fiduciary

BLACK & JONES
Attorneys at Law
30 Main Street
Anytown, U.S.A.

Harold H. Black
Gerald M. Jones

August 1, 19

Carter Insurance Agency
12 High Street
Anytown, U.S.A.

In re Estate of John W. O'Connor

Gentlemen:

This is to inform you that we have today filed
the final account in the above-captioned estate,
and that the bond of the fiduciary may be discon-
tinued.

Very truly yours,

BLACK & JONES

Harold H. Black

HHB:cn

FIGURE 3-3

Sample Letter Written Routinely by You
Enclosing Title Policy to Real Estate

BLACK & JONES
Attorneys at Law
30 Main Street
Anytown, U.S.A.

Harold H. Black
Gerald M. Jones

August 1, 19

Mr. & Mrs. Frederick T. Mullins
2972 Bricker Avenue
Anytown, U. S. A.

Dear Mr. & Mrs. Mullins:

Enclosed is a title policy issued by General American
Title Company, which insures you good title in the
new home you recently purchased.

The policy is a valuable document, and you should
keep it in a safe place.

I know that you both will enjoy our city.

Very truly yours,

BLACK & JONES

Harold H. Black

HHB:cn

Group #4: Requests for charitable donations and political campaigns can be presented to the attorney separately so that he may decide as to those to which he wishes to make contributions.

Group #5: If the employer's personal bills come to the office and if it is your job to see that they are paid, go over them carefully, verifying each expenditure, and pay particular attention to signatures on credit card purchases to make sure that they are the attorney's. If office invoices come to the attorney, verify these before they are paid. Paying office invoices is discussed in greater detail in Chapter Four.

Group #6: After you have been with your attorney for awhile, you will be aware of the type advertising he is interested in and you will be able to screen his mail for unwanted advertisements. You will know the type literature for law-book advertisements that he is interested in, and you will be able to determine what should and should not go into the waste basket.

Group #7: In handling checks for office fees or costs, you may separate all checks that come in the mail and, if you are also the bookkeeper, you may bank the checks in the proper account. This is discussed in greater detail in Chapter Four.

Of course, your method of handling the incoming mail is subject to the approval of the attorney, but following the above approach can save the attorney's time and spare him many details that do not require his attention, thus freeing his time for the more important legal matters that do require his specialized training.

The Tickler

Every law office needs at least one tickler or reminder system and each secretary should have her own. Certain duties need to be done on a recurring monthly basis, e.g., paying the parking lot for the attorney's monthly parking charge; paying the rent; paying rent for a ward; sending a monthly payment on a settlement in which your attorney has been made the trustee, and the money is to be disbursed monthly over a period of years (for instance, a bastardy settlement). For this type reminder system use a small, 3x5 card file and make a 3x5 card for each disbursement to be made. In the upper right hand corner put the day of the month the payment is due; further down on the card, type the description of the disbursement, to whom it is to be paid, how much, what for, payee's address and what account it is to be paid from. Use a set of indexes for 31 days of the month and file your cards behind the proper date. Each morning, your first duty is to remove the day's tickler cards and proceed.

Reminder systems can be set up for answer days, estate filings and filings of other necessary pleadings that have time limits. For this type reminder, you can use a whole year's set of monthly indexes with ample days of the month for each month. This would be a large file. Prepare cards in the same manner as described earlier and file

FIGURE 3-4

Sample Tickler Cards

```
                                              1st
   Mary M. Donovan Guardianship account

      Draw check to:

            Brown Management Co.
            30 N. Main Street       $120.00
            Any town, U. S. A.

         Rent for 1551 Euclid Avenue
                Any town, U. S. A.
```

```
                                           1st
   Draw check on Black & Jones Office Account

   in amount of $30

   Monthly parking
```

them in the appropriate month and day. As each day's ticklers are removed, place that day or month's index to the rear of the box, ready to come up in proper sequence. Place cards in the file a few days ahead of when they are due and use two or three reminder cards for each event, placing them at appropriate intervals with the final card under the due date.

The Appointment Calendar

There are many types of appointment calendars on the market, but the best is one that shows each day at a time and uses one side for appointments and the other side for reminders. This comes in a three-ring notebook and there is a junior size for the secretary. The supplier is Day-Timers, Inc., P.O. Box 2368, Allentown, Pa. 18001.

The attorney may authorize you to make all appointments for him as the clients call in for them. This sometimes requires skill and judgment in not placing appointments too closely together, allowing the attorney sufficient time for other appointments, meetings, lunch, etc. You should know something about the nature of the matter the client is coming in for so that you may judge the length of time required for the interview. This can usually be ascertained by a tactful, courteous "What type of matter is it, Mrs. Jones, so that I may know how much time to allow." Occasionally, a client will be reluctant to discuss his or her business with you; however, most clients will discuss these matters freely. The client need not be encouraged to go into great detail about his or her business with you; a general description of the matter is sufficient, such as a death in the family, buying or selling a home, etc.

Keep your calendar up to date with the attorney's so that you will be aware of who is coming in and can greet the client by name. This creates a pleasant client-secretary relationship.

Acting as a Witness for Wills
and Other Documents

One of your official duties may be to act as a witness on a will or other document such as a deed, mortgage, agreement, etc. When the attorney calls you into his office to act as a witness, you should sign your name in the proper place and then leave the office as soon as you have fulfilled your duty.

In some cases, such as that of the death of a person for whom you have witnessed a will, you may be called into court to swear that you witnessed the will, and you will be paid a fee for this service. On other occasions, such as in a will contest, you may be called to court to testify that the testator was of sound mind when he signed the will. If you do a lot of witnessing of wills and fear that you may not remember them all in case of a will contest, you might keep a file on all wills witnessed and jot down notes about the testator and the occasion of the signing of the will to refresh your memory. However, it is not likely that your attorney will permit any person he considers of unsound mind to make a will; therefore, you can be guided by this presumption.

Acting as a Notary Public

Notaries public have held office since the beginning of Christianity. In countries wherein Roman Law has prevailed, notaries public have had a greater variety of duties than in those countries wherein common law has been prevalent. In Civil Law, a notary public was known as registrarius, actuary, or scrivarius; he was a scribe who took notes and minutes and made drafts of writings. Presently, a notary public is usually one who merely attests to the genuineness of an instrument.

At one time, women were not eligible to become notaries public but, of course, in this modern age, women do hold the office.

Notaries public are usually limited to a specified territory, such as a county or a state, and are not authorized to act within any other jurisdiction. All states have statutes setting forth the powers of notaries public, and in no state do they have authority at common law.

A notary public cannot be held liable on his official bond for damages resulting from the signing of a jurat to an affidavit when he has knowledge that the affiant has sworn falsely. Usually, a notary public can be held liable only on the grounds of malice, corruption or negligence. For example, a notary public may be held liable for a false certificate of acknowledgement of a deed or mortgage or other instrument.

Usually, a notary public is required to use a seal to authenticate a document. In some states, it is required that the name of the notary public appear on his seal, and in some states it is required that the notary public must state the date of the expiration of his commission and typewrite or print his name underneath his signature.

Most notarizations in a law office consist of either a verification or an acknowledgement. A verification is usually used with court pleadings and consists of the affidavit of the client that the pleadings are true and correct. Following is an example:

STATE OF OHIO

COUNTY OF FRANKLIN, SS:

Mary D. Copeland, being first duly cautioned and sworn, deposes and says that the statements made in the foregoing petition and the allegations contained therein are true as she verily believes.

_____
Mary D. Copeland

Sworn to before me and subscribed in my presence this 1st day of August, 19___.

_____
Notary Public

You may have occasion to notarize verifications of this kind often. An acknowledgement is usually used on deeds and mortgages and may read as follows:

STATE OF OHIO, FRANKLIN COUNTY, SS:

BE IT REMEMBERED that on this_____ day of_____, 19___, before me, the subscriber, a Notary Public, in and for said County, personally came Mary D. Copeland the Grantor in the foregoing deed and acknowledged the signing thereof to be her voluntary act and deed.

IN TESTIMONY WHEREOF, I have hereunto subscribed my name and affixed my official seal on this day and year as aforesaid.

_____
Notary Public

The above acknowledgement is for an individual. An acknowledgement to be used for a corporation is as follows:

THE STATE OF OHIO, FRANKLIN COUNTY, SS:

BE IT REMEMBERED, that on this_____ day of_____, 19___, before me, the subscriber, a Notary Public in and for said County, personally came the above named THE L. B. SMITH COMPANY, by Robert J. Reed, its President, and Francis O. Scott, its Secretary, and as such President and Secretary duly authorized by resolution adopted by the Board of Directors of said Corporation, on the 1st day of August, 19___ acknowledged the signing of the same to be their voluntary act and deed for and as the act and deed of said Corporation, for the uses and purposes therein mentioned.

IN TESTIMONY WHEREOF, I have hereunto subscribed my name and affixed my official seal, on the day and year first aforesaid.

_____

Notary Public

Making Up a Form Book
for the Law Office

While each matter is an individual one and must be given individual attention, much legal work is repetitive and valuable time can be saved in the office by making up a loose-leaf notebook containing sample forms of work that is used constantly. The notebook can be a three-ring binder, using 8½x11 paper. The forms can be typed single-spaced to save space, even though the pleadings are usually double-spaced.

Divide the notebook according to the type of law involved, e.g., Probate, Domestic Relations, Real Estate, Trial Work, Corporate Work, and Miscellaneous forms. Enter the title of the form in the upper right hand corner of the page for the index, in caps and underlined. This title is not necessarily copied when the final draft is prepared; its use is for indexing only. Each form is given a number with a marking pen in the upper right hand corner, and each form is placed in a plastic sheet protector (available at any stationer). Also, make up an alphabetical index and a categorical index showing the number of each form. A certain number of pages should be assigned to each category, e.g., Probate, Domestic, etc., and those numbers should show in the index as belonging to that category.

You and the attorney can either use the same form book or one can be made up for each of you.

From the form book, it is a simple task for the attorney to dictate information, stating the paragraphs that you are to copy and then dictating the individual paragraphs that apply to the particular case.

Being a Personal Secretary

You may have personal duties to perform for your attorney. These duties should not be resented, but should be looked upon as a privilege—a privilege because your attorney trusts you and has

FIGURE 3-5

Sample Form from Form Book for Certifying
a Resolution of a Corporation

CERTIFICATE OF RESOLUTION

I, _____, Secretary of _____
(hereinafter called the Company), an Ohio corporation, do
hereby certify that at a special meeting of the Board of
Directors of said company, duly called and held on the 15th
day of October, 1971, the following resolutions were
adopted:

RESOLVED, That the Company shall convey title to
property located at 1371 S. Fourth Street,
Columbus, Ohio, to _____,
upon receipt of the amount of $4,148.70 plus interest
at the rate of 6½% from September 18, 1971, in
compliance with the terms of a land contract purchased
by the company.

FURTHER RESOLVED, that _____, President,
and _____, Secretary of the company
be and they hereby are authorized to execute and
deliver on behalf of the company a warranty deed
for said premises and to execute and deliver any
other instruments required by the company at the
closing of said real estate transaction.

And I do further certify that said resolution has not
been in any way amended, annulled, rescinded or revoked and
that the same is in full force and effect and that the same
does not and will not conflict with or result in any violation of any of the terms, provisions or conditions of
the Company's Articles of Incorporation, Code of Regulations
or of any existing contract or agreement to which it is a
party.

IN WITNESS WHEREOF, I have hereunto set my hand this
21st day of October, 1971.

                                    _____
                                               Secretary

FIGURE 3-6

Sample Categorical Index for Form Book

CORPORATION: Pages 41 through 50 inclusive
 Certificate of Resolution 41

PROBATE: Pages 1 through 20 inclusive
 Adoption, Final Degree of 1
 Adoption, Interlocutory Degree of 2
 Affidavit for Service by Publication 3
 Agreement re releasing administrator from liability 4
  when making distribution
 Attorney Fees, Application for Authority to pay & Journal
  Entry 5 and 5a
 Attorney Fees, consent to payment of 6
 Codicil 7
 Memorial, Application and Journal Entry re Authority
  to Purchase 8 and 8a
 Newly Discovered Assets, Journal Entry and Report 9 and 9a
 Release of Estate by Mortgagee 10
 Reopen Estate, Application and Journal Entry 11
 Service by Mail Clause 12
 Will 13
 Will, Contingent Executor Clause for 14
 Will, Life Estate Clause for 15
 Will, No-Contest Clause for 16
 Will, Simultaneous Death Clause for 17

REAL ESTATE: Pages 21 through 40 inclusive
 Affidavit for transfer of real estate on Auditor's
  Records 21
 Closing Statement 22
 Escrow Agreement 23
 Land Contract 24
 Land Contract, Release of 25
 Mortgage Note 26
 Mortgage Note with monthly reduction interest 27
 Mortgage, Partial Release of 28
 Title Opinion for abstract 29
 Title Opinion for title binder 30
 Warranty Deed, Exception Clause 31
 Warranty Deed, In compliance with land contract clause 32
 Warranty Deed, Joint and Survivorship Clause 33
 Warranty Deed, Life Estate Clause 34
 Warranty Deed, Mortgage Assumption Clause 35

enough confidence in you to take care of his very important personal affairs.

Some of the personal duties that you might be asked to perform are:

1. Paying household bills.
2. Maintaining a personal checking account.
3. Reminding him of important birthdays and purchasing birthday cards and gifts.
4. Shopping for his wife for such things as Valentine candy.
5. Christmas shopping.
6. Gathering data for income tax return.
7. Maintaining a register of insurance policies, securities owned, or real estate owned.
8. Preparing a financial statement of net worth.
9. Keeping vital statistics register.

Following are some pointers in performing the above personal duties.

PAYING HOUSEHOLD BILLS

If the attorney's household bills come to the office, keep a special file for them. Verify each bill as it comes in and, if necessary, or if there are any questions about the bill, check with the attorney or his wife to make sure that the item-in-question was ordered.

Pay each bill promptly, mark the date and check number on the bill and file it in a "paid-bill" file for future reference. The paid-bill file should be kept according to years. Arrange the bills in alphabetical order and clip them together in groups such as gas bills, electric bills, etc. The insurance-premium bills should be kept in one package so that they may be referred to readily. If the bills include a monthly mortgage payment, place a card in the tickler file so that the payment will be made when it is due.

MAINTAINING A PERSONAL CHECKING ACCOUNT

If the attorney asks you to keep a personal checking account for him, he may give you the authority to sign all checks on that account. If this is the case, maintain a complete record of each check that is written; the stubs can be invaluable at the end of the year for income tax records. Reconcile the account once a month with the bank statement and keep the canceled checks in a check file in numerical order so that they can be referred to, if necessary. Order checks and printed deposit slips as they are needed, and if the bank uses account numbers, you should verify the account number when the new checks and deposit slips are received. Make deposits of funds as the attorney so desires and keep a record of each deposit in the check book. In this way, a record of the attorney's income can be maintained and referred to at the end of each year (again for income tax purposes).

REMINDING HIM OF IMPORTANT BIRTHDAYS
AND PURCHASING BIRTHDAY CARDS AND GIFTS

If the attorney wants you to remind him of birthdays of his wife, children, grandchildren, and others, make up a 3x5 card for each birthday. Put the person's name and birthdate on the card (in the case of children, include the birth year). Arrange the cards numerically or chronologically and once every six months (or once a year); using your daily appointment calendar as a reminder, write in the birthdays two or three days ahead of time so that there will be ample time to purchase cards or buy gifts, particularly if they must be mailed. In the case of children, also write the current age on the calendar so that a special age card can be purchased for the child.

SHOPPING FOR HIS WIFE
FOR SUCH THINGS AS VALENTINE CANDY

Remind the attorney of important dates such as Mother's Day, Valentine's Day and Easter; he might wish to give his wife candy, a card, or some other gift. You may be asked to purchase the candy for him, and if you are, be sure to remind him to take it home that evening. Most wives will not resent this procedure since they will realize that their husbands have important details on their minds and may need reminding.

CHRISTMAS SHOPPING

If the attorney asks you to do some of his Christmas shopping, use your very best judgment in selecting items and do your best to please him.

FIGURE 3-7

Sample Cards from the Personal Tickler File

```
                                              1st
Draw check on Mr. Black's personal account

in amount of $162 to

        First Federal Savings & Loan Association


            Mortgage payment on house
```

```
                                          Feb. 12

Mr. Black's granddaughter's birthday
        February 14, 1960

        Pamela Sue Black
```

GATHERING DATA FOR INCOME TAX RETURN

At the end of the year, go through the check stubs in the personal checking account, starting at the beginning of the year, and make a list of all deductible items. To do this, use an 8½x11 sheet of paper, holding it sideways. Make headings for Medical, Drugs, Contributions, Interest Expense, Taxes, and Miscellaneous Deductions. Each time you come to a deductible item, list what the item is for and the amount under the appropriate column. When you have finished going through the entire year of check stubs, total the columns, and you

Sample Worksheet for Deductible Items for Homer J. Black's Income Tax Return

INTEREST		DOCTORS		PRESCRIPTIONS		DONATIONS		TAXES	
John Hancock	31.00	Drs. Breen & Hall	50.00	Halls Ph.	5.92	Fr. Law School	100.00	Real Est.	307.75
"	78.75	Fred M. Hunter, M.D.	30.00	Green Drugs	125.00	OSU Dev. Fund	10.00	City	
City Bank	16.00	James B. Horace "	255.00		130.92	YMCA	11.00		279.48
IRS	1.01	Blue Cross reimb.	181.00			Speech & Hg. Center	24.75	Real Est.	307.75
"	62.34	Hill, Carter & Jones, M.D.'s	6.00			OSU Assoc.	8.00		
Conn. Gen. Life	103.25	James R. Ford, M.D.	68.00			United Appeal	25.00		894.98
Mfrs. Life	10.18	John L. Gatsch, M.D.	10.00			Police Relief Fund	10.00		
Hunters Bank	2169.71	James R. Ford, M.D.	25.00			Junior Achievement	10.00		
First Nat. "	1193.51	James P. Fox, M.D.	9.00			Firemens Ben. Assoc	10.00		
" S&L	1671.78		453.00			Checkers Hockey Club	10.00		
	$5337.53	Less Blue Cross reimbursement	181.00				218.75		
			$272.00						

FIGURE 3-8

FIGURE 3-9

Sample Worksheet for Rental Property
for Homer J. Black's Income Tax Return

Property:			195 South Hudson Street
Gross rent received—19__			$1,170.00

Expenses:

Maintenance and Repair		Other	
Faucet handles	$ 2.80	Gas Co.	$ 81.00
Riser repair	40.13	Electric Co.	106.39
Toilet seat	3.38	Real Estate taxes	195.76
Keys & lock	5.00	Interest on	
Fixture	2.58	mortgage	1,264.89
Hauling trash	15.00	Management Fee	59.25
Repair gas leak	6.00		$1,707.29
Repair screen and			
plaster	20.00		
Replace storm door	44.50		
	$139.39		

	Gross Rent	$1,170.00
	Less expenses:	
	139.39	
	1707.29	1,846.68
	Loss	($676.68)

will have the amount for each type of deduction. This procedure will save the attorney hours of work. You can do the same thing with income, i.e., make headings for Income from Partnership, Salary, Dividend Income, Interest Income, Property Rental Income, etc.

MAINTAINING A REGISTER OF INSURANCE POLICIES, SECURITIES OWNED, OR REAL ESTATE OWNED

To keep track of the attorney's insurance program, take an 8½-x11 sheet turned sideways, and make headings: Company; Policy

Number; Inception Date; Term; Kind of Insurance; Person or Property Insured; Limits; Broker and Address. If the sheet is too crowded, you might use an 8½x14 sheet if your typewriter carriage is wide enough. Then, list the policies according to type of insurance, e.g., Life, Health and Accident, Home Owners, etc., giving the required information under each heading. The register will provide you or the attorney with a brief resume of all insurance, without looking at the actual policies, which may be kept in a safe deposit box.

The same procedure can be followed for securities or, if you prefer, you can use one of the many types of notebooks available in stationery stores for keeping track of securities.

This system is also conducive to keeping records of real estate and investment properties owned by the attorney. If the properties are handled by a management firm, keep a separate file for each property and in it keep the management firm's monthly report so that you will have a record of all income and expenditures on each property. (Again for income tax purposes and also for the attorney to be able to see if his investments are profitable.)

PREPARING A FINANCIAL STATEMENT OF NET WORTH

If you keep all the attorney's records, it should be an easy matter to prepare a financial statement for him if one is needed. He may wish to obtain a loan at the bank, or he may need such a record for other purposes. Simply list each asset, total, list each liability, total, deduct the liabilities from the assets, and the result is the attorney's net worth.

Insurance Register
Homer J. Black

Company	Policy No.	Inception date	Term	Kind of Ins.	Limits	Broker and Address
Mutual Life Ins. Co. of N.Y., The	5,000,000	11-14-40	Life	Ord. Life	$1,000 Db. Ind.	
Manufacturers Life Ins. Co., The	1,000,000	11-28-63	10 yr.	Term	$10,000	O'Harra Ins. Agency
Manufacturers Life Ins. Co., The	1,000,500	8-16-60	Life	Whole Life	$10,000	O'Harra Ins. Agency
Continental Assurance Co.	1,300,000	Oct. 23, 64	Life	Whole Life	7,500	
John Hancock Life Ins. Co.	6,000,500	12-20-55	Life		7,500	Wm. B. Johnson Agency
John Hancock Life Ins. Co.	1,999,999	5-31-31	66 yrs.		1,000	Wm. B. Johnson Agency
John Hancock Life Ins. Co.	2,000,339	5-18-34	63 yrs.		2,500 Disability Acc. Death $39,500	Wm. B. Johnson Agency
Miscellaneous:						
Conn. Gen. Life Ins.	MM-318390	2-9-62		Maj. Med.	Ded. $500 Max. $7,500	Ben Coulton Agency
Comm. Inc. Co. of Newark, N.J.	GX 9257	6-10-60		Loss of Income		Ben Coulton Agency
The Travelers Ins.	A(3)7316	9024-56		Loss of Income	L$125 2k.	
Conn. Gen. Life Ins.	661859	5-19-46		Family Income Plan	$25 wek. $60 mo.	Edw. D. Hannon
Buckeye Un. Fire Ins.	H329585	4-24-64	3 yrs.	Home Owners 350 Northview Dr. 195 S. Forest	$6,000	Herod Ins. Agency

KEEPING A VITAL STATISTICS REGISTER

It might be necessary from time to time to have information on hand concerning the attorney's personal statistics. This might be needed for the press or for various other purposes. To have this information handy, keep a list of such things as the attorney's birthdate, education, marital status, business or professional background, organizations to which he belongs, honors or achievements he has received, and hobbies.

FIGURE 3-11

Sample Financial Statement for Homer J. Black

ASSETS	
Residence: 350 Northview Drive	$35,000.00
1/2 interest in business building	27,500.00
Residence (rental property) 195 S. Hudson	17,500.00
Interest in Black & Jones	13,320.42
Interest in Black Real Estate Co.	11,000.00
Automobile, household furniture, etc.	5,000.00
Total assets	$108,320.44

LIABILITIES AND NET WORTH	
Mortgage indebtedness	$ 76,588.49
Charge accounts	375.00
Total Liabilities	$ 76,963.49
Homer J. Black, Net Worth	31,356.95
	$108,320.44

FIGURE 3-12

Sample Vital Statistics Data

Black, Homeı J.
Born: November 18, 1911
Wife: Grace Ann
Residence: 350 Northview Drive, Anytown, Ohio
Occupation: Attorney at law
Firm name: Black & Jones
Business address: 30 Main Street, Anytown, Ohio
Admitted to Bar: August 7, 1942
Member of Anytown Bar Association, Ohio State Bar Association,
    and American Bar Association

Politics: Republican

Education: Received BS in Business Administration 1933, Ohio
State University. Received LLB from Franklin University in 1942,
and Order of Curia. Received Juris Doctor Degree in 1966 from
Capital University. Wife, Grace Osborn, received BS in Education
from Ohio State University in 1934.

Children: Ruth, born Sept. 19, 1934. Now Mrs. James O'Connor, of
Los Angeles. Four children.
Homer J. Black, Jr., born Jan. 12, 1936, 2 children.

Mason Order—University Blue Lodge Chapter, Council, Commandry
    and Scottish Rite.

Board of Trustees, Anytown University, since 1944.

Member of North Avenue Methodist Church. Taught fourteen-year-
    old boys in Sunday School for fifteen years.

Kappa Sigma Fraternity.

Hobbies: Football games and fishing. Has attended every home
    game since 1923.

HOUSEKEEPING DUTIES

The amount of housekeeping duties required of you might depend
upon the type of janitor service available. If the janitor service is
weekly, you might be required to empty and wash ashtrays, empty

your waste basket, dust des¹ s and, occasionally, run a vacuum over soiled areas. If the janitor service is nightly, you will have little to do in the way of housekeeping, except to clean up your own desk at night and clean up the attorney's desk, if he so wishes. In cleaning up the attorney's desk, be careful not to disturb anything he might be working on at the moment. You can file away material that he is finished with and dust and arrange the desk neatly.

You might also be responsible for keeping the law library in order, returning books to their proper places on the shelves when they have been removed for research or placing new books on the shelves.

Last, but not least, if coffee is furnished, you may take care of making the coffee each morning, keeping the coffee station clean and offering coffee to clients in the waiting room.

Part of the qualifications for your job is the ability to know how to proceed in every circumstance that confronts you. It is a challenge to know where to turn at the appropriate time.

Keys to Efficient
Law-Office Management

Management duties are likely to be part of your daily routine and management ability is developed through insight, planning, experience and practice. This applies not only to management of the workload, but to management of people.

Some of the functions and processes of managing are: planning, initiating, decision-making, communicating and delegating.

To further identify these functions:

1. *Planning* defines goals and organizes resources toward achievement of goals. The planning process is dynamic.

2. *Initiating* gets resources organized and gives them a push—the energy to move.

3. *Decision-making.* The Western view of the manager places emphasis on speed in decision-making. A problem well defined is 90% of the way toward solution and a decision. There are three methods of decision-making: 1) complete; 2) act and report; and 3) act after approval. Ascertain which method you are authorized to use and act within the scope of the authority given you.

4. *Communicating* is fundamental to the management function. The normal result of human communication is partial misunderstanding, which is to some extent caused by preconceived ideas. Communication can be looked at from three points of view: sender—message—receiver. Good communicators analyze the role of the receiver.

5. *Delegating* is the direction and control of work activity and the means by which problems are solved. A person who knows how to delegate is an effective manager. You might ask, "Can a person manage an operation in which he does not know the technical details?" For a law office, this could mean, "Can a lay person manage a law office?" The answer is, "Yes," on the basis of what level technical decisions are necessary and what level management decisions are necessary. Motivation is also an important aspect of delegation. Some motivators are achievement, recognition, sense of responsibility, interest in the job and a sense of growth.

The most efficient and productive type of management is known as *Management-by-Objective*. This type of management states goals in such a way that they are measurable, scheduled and specific. It looks at results and it has confidence in people and their ability to accept responsibility. This is important because people are motivated when they feel a sense of responsibility. Thus, for the manager, knowledge of and insight into human behavior is a "must."

When it comes to human behavior, the subject of "role relationships" must be considered. Two people relating to each other are really playing eight roles; that is, each person plays the following roles:

1. How I see myself.
2. How I would like to be seen.
3. How I think I am seen.
4. How I am seen.

The greater the discrepancy between 1 and 2, the greater the difficulty. A person who sees himself as less than he would like is defensive. If there is a discrepancy between 2 and 3, it affects the evaluation of the other person.

Each of us plays three different roles:

1. Child role (present-tense oriented; emotional; not inhibited; will not take responsibility; is not creative).
2. Parent role (rules-and-regulations oriented, even though not realistic).
3. Adult role (reality-oriented at all times).

A parent-child relationship between a boss and a secretary is not a productive one and is not preferred by intelligent people. The best relationship is, of course, the adult-adult. However, nobody can play an adult role 24 hours a day. People always *need* other people.

Creativity is an important aspect of all functions of management. Solving problems can be done creatively with a six-step method:

1. Orientation and Definition. Defining and pointing-up the problem; listing related and sub-problems; clarifying the general problem situation.

2. Preparation. Gathering and analyzing pertinent data (facts, opinions, assumptions) about the problem.

3. Establishment of Alternatives. Developing as many alternatives and tentative ideas for solutions to the problem as possible; free-wheeling approach in which judgment is reserved.

4. Investigation and Insight. Investigating these alternatives, often followed by a period of incubation to let the ideas grow; ends in insight when the pieces fall into place.

5. Evaluation. Judging ideas based upon a set of criteria tailor-made to fit the particular problem situation.

6. Implementation. Developing a plan of action for carrying out the idea; selling the idea to those who must approve it and put it into effect.

Some of the other functions of management are:

1. Coaching and developing.
2. Coordination.
3. Facilities and equipment utilization.
4. Morale building.
5. Establishing priorities in work assignments.
6. Performance review.
7. Policies and procedures.
8. Self-development.
9. Work assignments.

Another important aspect of management is the use of leadership ability. The old-fashioned boss—known in the past for his coercive methods of threats of discharge, sarcasm and fault-finding to keep employees in line, domineering and impulsive tactics—is a thing of the past. This type boss' tools are fear and intimidation used to enforce blind obedience. Too many rules and regulations are a form of coercive bossing. Coercive bossing is, of course, a sign of emotional immaturity carried over from childhood.

Most people feel a psychological need to be led. Leadership is low-pressure not high-pressure.

Some of the traits most noted in people with leadership ability are:

1. Ability to make decisions.
2. Ability to assume responsibility without undue strain.
3. Sensitiveness to human traits and reactions.
4. Personal habits, appearance, and manner that build and maintain confidence.
5. Technical knowledge, experience, and training.
6. Integrity, fairness, and sincerity.
7. Forcefulness, energy, and perseverance.
8. Ability to inspire, teach, and develop people.
9. Power of analysis, discrimination of relative values.
10. Open-mindedness.
11. Tact and self-control.
12. Display of health and vigor stimulating to others.

Whether you have been given authority to organize your workload without supervision, or merely supervise one person, the above points can be applied.

Ordering Supplies

To you, particularly if you are in a smaller office, might fall the task of keeping the supplies of stationery in stock. When a number of people have access to the supplies, this can be a monumental task. Try to avoid that phrase, "We are out of the item."

You will probably develop your own system of knowing when to order and how much, but the following are a few basic points to remember:

1. Observe carefully for several months how long a particular item lasts. If the item goes pretty fast, increase the order the next time.

2. Encourage each member of the staff to let you know when an item is getting low, not when it is gone.

3. Inventory the stock periodically to see what is needed.

4. Keep the supply shelves in good order with all items of a kind together and always in the same place so they can be readily located.

5. Be sure that the storage shelves which hold the supplies are readily accessible and roomy.

6. Put marker stickers with the description of the item on the shelves underneath the items.

7. Take advantage of large-quantity ordering as much as possible, taking into consideration the amount of space available for storage of extra supplies.

8. For items that are printed, give the printer at least two weeks' notice. Better yet, check with the printer to see how much time he needs. There are many weights and types of papers and sizes and styles of printing. The following might be useful to bear in mind.

Letterheads can be ordered with 25% rag content, 50% rag content, 75% rag content, or 100% rag content, the latter being the best paper available. Second sheets for the business office range from 9 to 11 lb. in the onion skin and from 13 to 16 lb. bond paper. Bond papers may also be ordered in 20, 24, and 28 lb. for other purposes. Letterheads may be ordered in 8½x11 or the executive size, which is 7½x10½.

The common business envelopes are the No. 10, which is generally used for the 8½x11 letterhead, the executive size for the executive letterhead, and No. 6-3/4, which is the smaller letter envelope, and may be enclosed in a No. 10.

When ordering announcements, use an 8½x11 letterhead or the executive letterhead, or a panelled card known to printers as No. 5½. The Baronial is the most popular.

When ordering calling cards, order the standard size 3½x2. They may be ordered as translucent, thin plate, or vellum finish. For the attorney, Gothic letters in varied sizes and copper plate engraving is customary.

When material is received from the printer, verify it immediately for accuracy of the printing.

9. Compare prices with several firms to make sure you are getting the best price. (This will be sure to meet with the attorney's approval.)

10. Take into consideration the amount of delivery time required by each firm to whom orders are given, so that you can order well in advance.

11. Some items which are better priced or more suitable to the law office needs can be obtained from out-of-town suppliers. For this purpose it is convenient to keep an order book consisting of a three-ring notebook binder filled with plastic sheet protectors. Each sheet protector can contain order blanks, literature and other information for each supplier. An alphabetical index of supplies can be made up or an alphabetical list by items to be purchased may be kept, giving each a number. In the latter case, of course, it would be necessary to keep a numerical list also in order to keep track of numbers used.

FIGURE 4-1

Sample Index for Order Book

ALPHABETICAL INDEX

Amortization Tables 1
Brown Manila Envelopes, printed 3
Expanding Files 10
Corporate 4
Income Tax Blanks 5
Loan Payment Books 6
Receipt Books 7
Rubber Bands, large 8
Series E Bond Redemption Tables 2
Will Paper and Envelopes 9

NUMERICAL INDEX

1. Amortization Tables
2. Series E Bond Redemption Tables
3. Brown Manila Envelopes
4. Corporate
5. Income Tax Blanks
6. Loan Payment Books
7. Receipt Books
8. Rubber Bands, large
9. Will Paper
10. Expanding Files

12. Keep handy telephone numbers of all local suppliers.

13. Keep a memo of each item ordered and the date so that if the order doesn't arrive in a reasonable time, you can check it. Then, too, when the order does arrive you can use this list to verify actual receipt of the items.

14. Check invoices when they are received against delivery slips to make sure the billing does not include an item not received.

15. Check packages as they are received against the delivery slips to make certain everything listed is enclosed.

16. Keep a lookout for new products that will increase efficiency in the office.

17. Check with all personnel to ascertain personal preferences of different types of items and try to order to please as many persons as possible.

18. Be sure to conform to the policies of the attorney.

19. When ordering carbon paper, first determine the number of copies which will be required and order the proper weight. Carbon papers come in the following weights:

> 4 lb.-light—makes 1-12 copies
> 5 lb.-medium—makes 1-7 copies
> 8 lb.-standard—makes 1-4 copies

The lightweight actually only makes about 1-9 copies, the way present-day manufacturers are making it. Manufacturers are following the trend to the use of copy machines for multiple copies and may completely eliminate the medium weight. More and more offices are finding it practical to use copy machines when more than four copies are needed, and some offices have eliminated carbon papers altogether.

20. When ordering file folders, be sure to specify the size and cut of tab. File folders come in letter, legal, invoice, check, jumbo, and tab sizes.

> Invoice size—9-3/4x7½
> Check size—9x4
> Jumbo size—17-4/5x14½
> Tab size—7-3/8x3/4

Folders may be ordered according to the size of the tab for indexing as follows:

1/3 cut
1/5 cut
2/5 cut—right of center
2/5 cut right position
2/5 right position undercut
2/5 cut right also comes with printed lines.

Also available are Guide Heights folders, which are taller than standard files, and folders with side tabs for vertical files with various color codings.

The invoice size may be ordered in 1/2 and 1/3 cuts; the check size in 1/2, 1/3 and 1/4 cuts; the jumbo size comes in square and half cut; and the tab size comes only in square cut.

21. When ordering pencils be sure to specify the type graphite desired, i.e. soft, hard, medium.

Keeping in mind the above basics, you should be able to keep the supply flowing smoothly and there shouldn't be any ruffled tempers at finding an item out of stock.

Legal blanks can be stocked in the same manner.

Organizing the Workload

If the lawyer authorizes you to organize your own workload with little or no supervision, you should have an in-basket technique. A file basket on your desk would hold incoming work for the day, whatever the source. Early in the day or perhaps several times a day you should go through the basket for first-priority items. Perhaps the lawyer has given you a job which he wants done right away. That is top priority. The work can be arranged in the order of imperativeness. Work right down through the basket in priority order. If work is held over until the next day its priority can be rescheduled with newly received work.

To facilitate dictation, the attorney may have a dictation basket on his desk and any matter that arises requiring dictation may be placed into the basket until the dictation period. From time to time files may come first to your attention requiring the lawyer's dictation. These may be placed in the dictation basket.

Place another file basket convenient to the lawyer so that he may place file material in it to be filed regularly at your convenience.

FIGURE 4-2

Sample Order in which Work Basket Could Be
Placed (Arranged) for the Day on Monday

1. Title opinion to be typed for 3 p.m. closing.

2. Tape with three letters to be ready by 5 o'clock.

3. Will to be ready by 10 a.m. tomorrow morning.

4. Abstract continuation and deed to be ready by
    tomorrow afternoon.

5. Title opinion to be ready for Friday closing.

6. Final account in an estate to be gotten ready
    as soon as possible.

7. Divorce pleadings to be ready for signature
    by Friday afternoon.

8. Type up some new forms for form book in spare time.

Supervising the Junior Secretary

If you are a senior secretary you usually are able to give your overload to a junior secretary who perhaps does not have the workload that you have. In this case, delegate work according to the degree of experience and scope of the junior secretary. She may be trained to do jobs that have not come within her experience. Proofread work done by a junior secretary. You are responsible for all work done in this matter.

Supervision is an art, requires some insight into psychology of human relations, and should be worked at. The following guidelines may be useful in supervising.

Do . . .

1. Show appreciation for a job well done.
2. Set a high standard of requirements of work, but don't expect the impossible

3. Treat people for their individual worth regardless of level—social, professional, education, or prestige of position.
4. Be fair in resolving problems, using good judgment.
5. Keep employees informed on office matters and respect their ability to keep such matters confidential when they should not be discussed.
6. Respect employees' opinions; ask for their opinions on office matters.
7. Take a personal interest in employees.
8. Make no greater demands on the employees than you do of yourself. Adhere to office rules and regulations the same as other employees must do.
9. Show your confidence.
10. Be loyal to the employees.
11. Display organizational ability.
12. Maintain a good sense of humor.
13. Be considerate of employees' personal time, never asking for extra hours without checking to make sure it doesn't interfere with important personal plans.
14. Give verbal recognition for special services.

Don't . . .

1. Put a round peg in a square hole.
2. Spend too much time on a few matters and let other things pile up.
3. Procrastinate.
4. Be unclear in communication, or expect employees to be mind readers. This results in the duplication or omission of work.
5. Be wordy in written communications.
6. Give too much detailed instruction. This robs an employee of initiative.
7. Be impatient.
8. Show a passionate dislike for details and not wish to be bothered with them.
9. Be unappreciative of the amount of time it takes to get things done. This results in too much rush work.
10. Call out instructions without waiting for the employee to get into your office.

Banking Fees

If you are a managing secretary you may be in charge of collecting, recording, and banking the fees of the firm. There are many systems available and some specifically geared to attorneys. The attorney may have his favorite system already set up or may be open to a new one. Whatever system is used, you should record the fees and whatever information might be required by the bookkeeping system in use, such as which attorney is responsible for the fee, what type of matter the fee is for; i.e., Domestic, Probate, Real Estate, Trial Work, Personal Injury Suit, etc. The fees should be deposited in the office checking account at regular intervals. Be very careful to distinguish between fees, court costs deposited, and trust monies.

FIGURE 4-3

Sample Deposit Record of Fees Banked

11-1-

Nina Masters, Divorce, H. J. Black	$ 250.00
Nina Masters, return of costs advanced	25.00
Estate of Sanford J. Rousch, Probate, HJB	1,000.00
Estate of Sanford J. Rousch, return of costs advanced	90.00
Henry Holman, purchase of residence, GMJ	100.00
	$ 1,465.00

Paying Accounts Payable

The accounts payable to the firm should be accumulated for a month in a special folder in alphabetical order and paid by the tenth of the month following the one in which they were received. Accounts should be verified before they are paid. Check stationery and supply invoices against delivery slips for accuracy. When the bills are paid, make notation of the date, amount, and check number on the invoice, and place them in a special file. This can be an expanding pocket file, with an alphabetical index of pockets. At the end of the year date the file for the year and store it. The invoices can be destroyed at the end of the statutory limit period for open accounts in the state in which the firm operates. Keep invoices for capital expenditures which are depreciated, such as furniture and equipment, in a special file and preserve them.

Care of Equipment

Record the serial numbers of all typewriters, adding machines, calculators, etc. in an appropriate place for several reasons—for depreciation purposes, or in the event of a burglary so that the equipment can be identified by police. All typewriters and calculators should be covered with dust covers at night before leaving the office.

Usually typewriters are under maintenance agreements and a repairman may be called at any time without charge, except for replacement of certain parts. Keep the names and telephone numbers of repairmen used in a handy place.

If the firm uses copy equipment of some sort, you probably will be the "key operator." You will clean the drum, put in the toner and check the machine to see that it is operating properly.

If a Xerox machine is leased you must read the meter or meters on the last day of the month and send in the report to the company for billing. You should keep your own record of meter readings and check it against the invoice when it comes in. Keep the paper, toner, and cleaning fluid and cotton well stocked so that you will not run out of these items, and clean the drum regularly, if you have a model which requires drum cleaning.

Human Relations in the Law Office

Wherever you find two people you find human relations. The law office spends its time trying to solve the problems of people, and therefore, its internal organization should run smoothly. This section will attempt to point out some methods of aiding human relations in the law office.

FRANKNESS IN TALKING OVER PROBLEMS
BETWEEN THE LAWYER AND YOU

"He made me mad, and I told him off and walked out," vehemently spoke Anne as she lunched with Kathy. Anne was talking about her lawyer-boss and that day's event was the culmination of months of resentment Anne had built up about the law firm she worked for—too much work, no help, etc. Had Anne been frank with her attorneys and at least tried to talk over her resentments as they arose, perhaps this little story would never have unfolded.

Most lawyers will talk things over. After all that is their business—to talk over troubles with their clients, so why wouldn't they extend a sympathetic ear to you?

Compatability plays a big role in frank talks. You and your boss must establish a kind of rapport to work together harmoniously. Psychology tells us that "exact alikes" do not always work out the best because although they work more harmoniously, and have less friction, it is more difficult for them to make achievements. The magic formula is a proper balance of mutual interests and individual differences.

The individual differences shouldn't be in the form of set viewpoints to create friction, but should be in abilities. Just as a partnership succeeds if one man is capable in one area and another in a different area of practice, a secretary-boss relationship is a partnership, and you, being the junior partner, meaning that you play a minor role in the decision- and policy-making as compared to the senior partner, your boss, draw a smaller percentage of the profits in the way of salary, and your investment of capital is your ability and skill which you place at the advantage of the partnership. This team of boss and secretary should face the clientele and the rest of the office force with a united front.

Another way of looking at a boss-secretary team is to compare it to an agency. The duties owed by an agent to his principal can very well be applied to you. Let's examine them.

THE DUTY TO BE LOYAL

Just as the agent owes a duty to his principal to be loyal to his interests at all times, so must you be loyal at all times to your boss if a good working relationship is to be established. You must defend and practice the policies set up by your employer. You must guard his confidential files zealously from those not concerned and place the affairs of his practice before your own personal affairs.

THE DUTY TO CARRY OUT INSTRUCTIONS

An agent must carry out the instructions of his principal or he may become personally liable to a third party with whom he is contracting. You are under a duty to carry out the instructions of your employer, assuming, of course, that your employer is not operating in an illegal manner and does not request any immoral act or any act against the law. Of course, unusual circumstances may arise when previous instructions would be detrimental to the interest of the employer and as in the case of an agent, you must exercise your best judgment if the employer is not available.

THE DUTY NOT TO BE NEGLIGENT

An agent implies that he has the necessary skill and training to perform an agreed task. When you agree to accept a certain position you are implying that you have the training and skill necessary to competently discharge the duties of the position. While you may not be liable for money damages as the result of a negligent act on your part wherein your employer paid money to a third party, as is the agent, you nonetheless have a duty to your attorney-employer to perform competently and not cause your attorney any loss through negligent acts on your part.

THE DUTY TO ACCOUNT

An agent is required by law to make an accounting of any funds he collects for his principal. You owe a duty to your employer if you handle his funds and collect any monies for him, to keep proper records and make an accurate accounting of all monies received and disbursed by you.

THE DUTY TO DISCLOSE FACTS

An agent must report to his principal any fact that comes into his possession which might materially affect the principal's interest or any conflicting interest of a third party with whom the agent might be dealing on behalf of the principal. You also have a moral obligation to disclose any pertinent information which might come to your attention if the facts so learned would in any way affect your attorney-employer's interests.

PSYCHOLOGICAL APPROACH TO PROBLEMS IN RELATIONSHIPS WITH OTHER EMPLOYEES

The most nearly perfect rule of conduct that man has come up with so far is the Golden Rule, "Do unto others as you would have others do unto you." This rule should be followed in office relationships. Some of the Do's and Don'ts that might be considered using the Golden Rule are as follows:

Do . . .

1. Give your attorney-employer a full day's work for a full day's pay.
2. Confine your lunch hour to the time allotted.
3. Take pride in the neatness and accuracy of the work you turn out.
4. Dress appropriately and neatly. If your office permits pants suits, do wear attractive, two-piece suits, *not* slacks and assorted tops and sweaters. Abide by your employer's wishes with regard to minis, midis, and maxis.
5. Observe prompt starting time and do not object to staying a few minutes past quitting time, if necessary.

Don't . . .

1. Criticize your fellow employees in a negative, destructive manner.
2. Talk about your fellow employees behind their backs, unless what you say is complimentary.
3. Ask a co-worker to help you with your work if you wouldn't do the same for her.
4. Be late coming back from lunch, especially if lunch hours are staggered, and delay the next girl's lunch hour.
5. Carry off pencils, erasers, paper clips, and other supplies belonging to your employer for your personal use.
6. Overdo the personal phone calls. Your employer's phone is for his business calls and your time belongs to him.

7. Take prolonged coffee breaks. A break is refreshing and increases efficiency, but if overdone encroaches on the boss's time.

THE EXPERIENCED SECRETARY AND THE NEW ASSOCIATE OR LAW CLERK

If you have been on the job many years you may be an authority on procedure. The young law clerk or young associate just fresh out of law school is well versed in theory of law, but usually knows less than you might about practical procedure.

In this case, you should give the young clerk or associate the respect that is due him and tactfully point out procedure to him whenever it is necessary.

Setting Up a Trust Account for Clients' Funds

Since clients often pay funds to the attorney to be forwarded to others, e.g., to Clerk of Courts for court costs, alimony payments to a spouse and attorney, or monies to be held for a few months, such as estate funds, a separate account for these funds must be set up. It is unethical for an attorney to commingle this type of fund with his own funds. If you handle trust monies be extremely careful with records and disburse the funds only at the direction of the attorney responsible, and for the purpose intended, lest the attorney be accused of mishandling funds. Funds should be disbursed from this account up to the amount deposited. Do not make advancements on this account.

A simple, effective method of recording trust funds is to use a small card file for 3x5 cards. Using an alphabetical index guide make a 3x5 account card for each client depositing funds, with columns for debits, credits, and balance. Each card should be marked "Trust Account" in case it should become mixed up with other cards. The client's last name should come first. The name or initials of the attorney who is responsible for the funds should also be placed on the card.

As funds come into the account or are disbursed from it, enter them immediately. Part of the essence of the system is its "instant" reference. At any moment you should be able to determine how much is in a client's trust fund.

FIGURE 4-4

NAME		ADDRESS		FILE NO.	
Fawcett, Robert		HM3	Trust Acct.		
DATE	ITEM	DEBITS	CREDITS	BALANCE	
		Receipts	Disb	Bal.	
8-1-	Robert Fawcett	5900 00			
8-1-	Franklin Co. Aud.				
	Transfer Tax		590		
	The H. W. Garden Realty				
	Co.,real estate				
	commission		35400		
	H. O. Sands, Seller		554010	000	

When the funds are disbursed, remove the card from the file and place it in another file for storage. It can be pulled if the same client again brings in funds.

Once a month the trust account check balance should be reconciled with the bank statement, and the balances on all cards should be totalled and should equal the current balance in the checking account. This is a double check on the accuracy of record keeping.

FIVE

Effective Filing Techniques
in the Law Office

The importance of a good, adequate filing system from which records may be immediately retrieved cannot be too strongly emphasized. Records are useless if they cannot be located when needed. Your office may find that an alphabetical system is sufficient, or that a combination alphabetical system and numerical system might better suffice, and perhaps going even further, a subjective and categorical file might be useful.

In addition, many subsidiary filing systems are useful, such as a special file for legal blanks to help in fast retrieval, a special alphabetical file for wills, or a special file for retaining abstracts of title for clients, or a special file for locating and retaining continuations of abstracts of title. All of these filing methods are discussed in the following pages, along with some guides for filing supplements to reference books, such as Prentice-Hall's Tax Guide and Wills and Trusts Service.

The Alphabetical File

Most material can be filed alphabetically. Being thoroughly familiar with the alphabet is the main requirement for this type of filing. Labels can be placed on the file folders, with the last name of the client first and filed in that order. Many attorneys prefer to handle their current cases in this manner.

The larger the filing system the more subheadings would be required under each letter of the alphabet. For example, under the letter B, tabs could be inserted marking the beginning of the BEs or the BRs. Use as many tabs as the size of the filing system seems to require.

Local telephone directories are excellent sources of reference to check on the proper listing of alphabetical sequences. However, if your local telephone directory does not solve the problem you may write to System Service Department, Oxford Filing Supply Co., Inc., East Stewart Avenue, Garden City, N.Y. 11530.

For the New York City directories, the telephone company requires 15 pages of rules to govern precedence of listing; however, most situations can be covered by the following simple rules:

1. File each name in the exact sequence of its letters—maintain alphabetic sequence to the last letter of the word.

2. Consider last names first, then given names, then initials. Complete each unit before going on to the next. Remember that "Nothing comes before something." (Johnson, Joseph comes before Johnson, Joseph A.)

3. Abbreviations of first names of individuals are indexed and filed as though written in full. (Chas. is filed as Charles.)

4. Names beginning with M', Mac or Mc should be listed in order as spelled and treated as one word, thus, MacDonald, Mansfield, Mc-Call, M'Donald.

5. Titles and degrees whether preceding or following the names are disregarded. (Lt. Col. A.H. Jameson would be filed as Jameson, A.H., Lt. Col.)

RULES FOR COMPANY, INSTITUTION AND GOVERNMENT NAMES

1. To index a company named after an individual, arrange the name by units as with individual names. Thus: G.S. Crane and Company would be indexed: Crane, G.S., and Company.

2. File coined or trade names without rearrangement. (Vic Tanny as Vic Tanny; Oxford Filing Supply Company, Inc. as written.)

3. When initials comprise a firm name, treat them as a single unit. (WOR, as such.)

4. To prevent filing errors, write out abbreviations. Thus,

Y.M.C.A. should be written out in full and filed as such. File abbreviations for cities and states as if they were spelled out. (N.Y. would appear before North Carolina.)

5. Papers or letters from national, state, county, or city governments should be filed under the name of the nation, state, county, or city—and then by department or bureau in alphabetical order. In such cases the words "Bureau of" or "Dept. of" should be disregarded in determining the sequence.

The Categorical File

Many attorneys find it convenient to file alphabetically by type of case matter. For instance, one drawer could be labelled "Litigation" and all cases in litigation could be filed in that drawer alphabetically. Another drawer could be labelled "Pending real estate closing" and another "Simple Wills." Another could be labelled "Estate Plans," another "Estates," and another "Income Tax Returns," another "Guardianships" and finally a "Miscellaneous" drawer.

To retrieve the file all that is needed is to know the type of matter involved. Usually you and your attorney, if there is not an overload of cases, will be familiar with clients' cases. Each of the categorical files should contain its own alphabetical set of index cards.

THE SIMPLE WILL FILE

It is expedient to keep copies of simple wills made for clients in their own file. This can be done alphabetically using an alphabetical set of indexes, placing behind the letter of the alphabet a legal size file folder labelled "Simple Wills—A" etc. File copies of wills of all clients whose last names begin with A in the A folder and so on down through the alphabet.

THE ESTATE PLAN FILE

For the clients who have complicated estate plans and testamentary or inter-vivos trusts (described in Chapter Six) it is best to keep an individual file folder for each client containing copies of whatever documents have been drawn. Label these folders with the client's name and mark them "Estate Plan" so that they will get into the proper file, then file them alphabetically in their own drawer.

Closed Files and the Numerical System

When a case is finished the file must be stored in case it is needed sometime in the future. To simplify storage of closed files a numerical system of filing may be used in conjunction with an alphabetical card file. As each file is closed, give it a number. Stamp the number on the file tab with a number stamp and at the same time, on a 3x5 card with client's name on it. File the 3x5 cards alphabetically and use them to locate the file by client. When the file is needed, get the number of the file from the card and retrieve that numbered file from the numerically filed cabinet. If the client has more than one matter or file, the files can be numbered 1 A, 1 B, 1 C, etc.

A running numerical control guide should be kept so that there will be a record of the last number used and the client to whom each number is assigned. This can be kept in a small three-ring notebook. This notebook also can be used to locate a file which was not indexed properly.

FIGURE 5-1

Numerical Index—Closed Files

1. Jones, James P.

2. Brown, Jack L.

3. Smith, George R.

4. Kennedy, Lulu P.

5. Camper, Bruce L.

Alphabetical Card—Closed Files

Jones, James P.

Subject File for Reference Materials

Sometimes small booklets and pamphlets which an attorney sometimes refers to will accumulate in his office. These can best be kept in a subject file, classified by subject matter. First group them together according to subject matter, then assign each subject a number in sequence, perhaps with subnumbers under each main category. Make up a numerical index and also an alphabetical index for easy finding. From your stationer's you can obtain files with upright tabs for inserting typewritten headings. Type the number and classification on each tab and file the pamphlets accordingly in file folders. Mark each pamphlet with its proper number to facilitate refiling after usage.

FIGURE 5-2

Alphabetical Index—Subject File

Accounting, tax 1
Antitrust Laws 2
Back Injury Cases 3
Corporations, Collapsible 4
Equipment Leasing 5
Estates: 6
    Contests 6.1
    Defamation Actions 6.2
    Estate Administration (Contests) 6.6
    Estate Planning 6.3
    Tax Factors 6.4
    Wills & Trust Agreements 6.5
Federal Taxes: 7
    American Bar Bulletins 7.1
    Buying & Selling a Business 7.2
    Code of 1954 7.3
    Corporate 7.4
    Current Problems 7.5
    Deductions and Credits 7.6
    Depreciation 7.7
    Employee Stock Options 7.8

Enrollment Examination 7.9
Entertainment Industry 7.10
Estates & Trusts 7.11
Farmer 7.32
Federal Tax Guide (Prentice-Hall) 7.12
Federal Tax Report (Commerce Clearing House) 7.13
General 7.14
Gift 7.15
Income Averaging 7.16
Individual 7.17
Installment Sales 7.18
Marital Deduction 7.19
Multiple Corporation 7.20
Partnership 7.21
Penalty Taxes 7.22
Personal Holding Companies 7.23
Private Foundations 7.24
Procedure 7.25
Publications 7.26
Real Estate 7.27
Revenue Act of 1964 7.28
Small Business 7.29
Travel & Entertainment Deductions 7.30
Withholding Tables 7.31
Ford Foundation 8
Housing Code of Columbus 9
Inheritance Tax 10
Juvenile Court 11
Kiplinger Washington Letter 12
Lawyers' Weekly Report 13
Maps & Travel 14
Ohio National Bank Letter 15
Ohio State Bar Association Letter 16
Oil & Gas Leasing 17
Personal Property Tax 18
Protecting Trade Secrets 19
Real Estate: 20
    Abstracting & Title Search 20.1
    Land Plotting Charts 20.12
    Legislation 20.3
SEC Rules 21
Secured Transactions 22
Self-Employed Tax Saving Plans 30
Social Security 23

Stocks: 24
  Moody's Annual Dividend Record 24.1
  Mutual Funds 24.2
  Stock Values & Yields 24.3
Subdivision Regulations, Franklin County 25
Support, Mental Institutions, Ohio 29
Trust Agreement (Revocable Insurance) 26
Unemployment Compensation 27
Uniform Commercial Code 28

Numerical Index—Subject File

1. Accounting, tax
2. Antitrust Laws
3. Back Injury Cases
4. Corporations, Collapsible
5. Equipment Leasing
6. Estates:
    1. Contests
    2. Defamation Actions
    3. Estate Planning
    4. Tax Factors
    5. Wills & Trust Agreements
    6. Estate Administration (Contests)
7. Federal Taxes:
    1. American Bar Bulletins
    2. Buying & Selling a Business
    3. Code of 1954
    4. Corporate
    5. Current Problems
    6. Deductions and Credits
    7. Depreciation
    8. Employee Stock Options
    9. Enrollment Examination
    10. Entertainment Industry
    11. Estates & Trusts
    12. Federal Tax Guide (Prentice-Hall)
    13. Federal Tax Reports (Commerce Clearing House)
    14. General
    15. Gift
    16. Income Averaging
    17. Individual
    18. Installment Sales

19. Marital Deduction
20. Multiple Corporations
21. Partnership
22. Penalty Taxes
23. Personal Holding Companies
24. Private Foundations
25. Procedure
26. Publications
27. Real Estate
28. Revenue Act of 1964
29. Small Business
30. Travel & Entertainment Deductions
31. Withholding Tables
32. Farmer
8. Ford Foundation
9. Housing Code of Columbus
10. Inheritance Tax
11. Juvenile Court
12. Kiplinger Washington Letter
13. Lawyers' Weekly Report
14. Maps & Travel
15. Ohio National Bank Letter
16. Ohio State Bar Association Letter
17. Oil & Gas Leasing
18. Personal Property Tax
19. Protecting Trade Secrets
20. Real Estate:
    1. Abstracting & Title Search
    2. Land Plotting Charts
    3. Legislation
21. SEC Rules
22. Secured Transactions
23. Social Security
24. Stocks:
    1. Moody's Annual Dividend Record
    2. Mutual Funds
    3. Stock Values & Yields
25. Subdivision Regulations, Franklin County
26. Trust Agreement (Revocable Insurance)
27. Unemployment Compensation
28. Uniform Commercial Code
29. Support, Mental Institutions, Ohio
30. Self-Employed Tax Savings Plans

The Form File for Legal Blanks

Most law offices use a certain amount of printed blank forms, merely filling in the blanks. Unless these are kept in an orderly fashion, they become difficult to use. Place each type of blank in a legal size folder, labelled as to its contents and placed in an alphabetical file just for that purpose.

FIGURE 5-3

List of Labels for Form File

Accounts, Probate
Administrator, Application for
Affidavit of Residence & Debt (Sale of Stock)
Appraisers, Probate
Attorney Fees, Probate, Application and J.E.
Auto Accident Report
Auto Title Forms

Bankruptcy, Proof of Claim
Bills of Sale
Birth Certificates, Application for
Blue Cross Applications
Bond, Probate

Change of Name
Closing Statements
Cognovit Notes
Consent of Heirs to Take Real Estate
Commissioner, Appointment of
Corporation, Articles of
Corporation, Dissolution
Corporation, Minute Paper
Corporation, Stock Certificates

Deeds, Admr. & Exec.
Deeds, Admr. & Exec., Under Authority of Will
Deeds, Corporate
Deeds, Guardianship
Deeds, Mortgage
Deeds, Quit Claim
Deeds, Trustee
Deeds, Warranty, Long form
Deeds, Warranty, Short form

Deeds, Warranty, Statutory
Deposition, Notice to Take
Distribution in Kind, Probate

Election of Surviving Spouse
Employer's Identification Number, App. (Federal)
Employer's Withholding Exemption Certificates (Federal)
Escrow Agreement
Estate Tax, Federal
Estate Tax, Ohio
Eviction Notice
Executor, Application for, Probate
Extension of Time, Probate

Financial Responsibility
Forcible Entry and Detention

Guardian Ad Litem
Guardianship Forms

Hearing Date, Entry Setting, Probate

Insurance Forms
Interview Sheet for Estates
Inventory
Inventory, Trustee's

Land Contracts
Leases
Liquor Permit Applications

Marriage Licence Application for Copy
Mechanic's Lien Affidavit
Medical Authorization
Medicare Forms

No Administration
Notice of Will filed for Probate

Paternity, Declaration of

Real Estate Purchase Contract
Release of Estate of Mortgagee
Retainer Agreement
Sale of Personal Property, Probate
Sale of Real Estate, Probate
Schedule of Debts, Probate
Security Agreement
Seller's Affidavit

Social Security
Stock Powers
Stock Valuation Forms

Transfer Auto, Probate
Transfer of Real Estate, Probate
Trustee, Appointment of

Uniform Dependency Act

VA Claim Forms

Wills, Application to Admit
Wills, Deposit of
Wills, Foreign, Admit to Probate
Workmen's Compensation

The Abstract File

Clients often do not have a place to keep an abstract and they will ask the attorney to keep it for them. A special file drawer can be set aside for them and equipped with a set of alphabetical index guides. Place each abstract in a large manila envelope, labelled with the client's name and the address of the real estate and placed alphabetically in the abstract file. Thus, if a client inquires as to whether the attorney is keeping his abstract, or if he wishes to take it home with him, it can be readily located.

The Abstract Continuation File

Many firms do abstracting, and a problem may arise as to how to file abstract continuations. Assign a special drawer for these. Number the abstract continuations and type the number on the tail sheet at the bottom. Keep a running index of numbers showing the name of the client (similar to the one for closing files) and an alphabetical list for quick locating. This can all be done in a small notebook equipped with an alphabetical index. When a continuation is completed and the next number assigned to it, place it in the running numerial list, and put the client's name in the alphabetical section of the notebook with the assigned number typed after it. The copies of the continuations may then be kept in legal size folders (50 to the folder) and the folders labelled 1-50, 51-60, etc.

Filing Supplements to Reference Materials
and Tax Guide Materials

If the attorney subscribes to supplement services for such reference materials as Tax Guides and Will Files or receives regular supplements to other volumes in his library such as the state code etc., keep them up to date.

It is important to read the instructions that come with the supplements as in some cases you will destroy the old supplements and in some cases you will retain them.

In the case of loose-leaf pages to be substituted for various other pages, the instructions will tell you which to discard and which to insert. Usually there is a long list of page numbers and it is best to use a ruler to run across the lines so as to avoid picking up a number from the next line and thus shuffling the pages. Another danger is in misreading the numbers, such as 10,280 might be erroneously filed in the 10,380 group. Exercise great care in reading the number properly. It is very important to the attorney that these pages are correctly filed, for when he researches a problem he may be thrown completely out of line if one page is in the wrong place.

The law office that has a place for everything and everything in its place will attract clientele.

SIX

You and Probate Law

Probate Law may vary from state to state. However, certain generalities prevail, and the following pages may be helpful to you if your attorney specializes in Probate Law. If you are knowledgeable in Probate Law procedures you can be a right arm to your attorney.

The Will

Since the laws of intestate succession will apply if an individual dies intestate (without a will), and since the laws do not always distribute the deceased's property as he would have wished (see the table on page 82 showing the order of relationship to decedent), most people make a will. Whether it is a simple will or a complex trust will depend on the amount of assets that the testator has.

THE SIMPLE WILL

The simple will is as its name implies, simple in nature. It may consist of a few specific bequests with the residuary estate going to another person and close with the appointment of an executor who may be given full powers in administering the estate. A simple will for a married couple with children usually amounts to each leaving his or her estate to the other, or in the event of the death of both, to their children, equally share and share alike on a per stirpes basis. The simple will may include a pretermitted heir clause (referring to children born to the testator after the will is executed) and conclude with the appointment of each partner as the other's executor or executrix.

FIGURE 6-1

THE STATUTE OF DESCENT AND DISTRIBUTION
Revised Code of Ohio, Section
2105.06

There are important exceptions to this general
statutory provision.

WHEN A PERSON DIES WITHOUT A WILL, PROPERTY DESCENDS AND
IS DISTRIBUTED AS FOLLOWS:

Widow or Widower with Child, Children or
Descendants:

All to Child or Children Divided Equally

Grandchildren take their deceased parent's
share.

Married Man or Woman With Child, Children
or Descendants:

Two or More Children

Wife or Husband One-Third

Children Two-Thirds, divided equally

Grandchildren take their deceased
parents share

One Child Only

Wife or Husband One-Half

Child One-Half

Grandchildren take their
deceased parent's share.

Married Man or Woman without Child, Children,
or Descendants:

If Parents Survive

Wife or Husband Three-Quarters

Parents or Survivor One Quarter

No Parents Surviving

Wife of Husband
takes all Property

Unmarried Man, Woman, Widow or Widower
Without Children or Descendants:

If Parents Survive

All to Father and Mother,
or Survivor

No Parents Surviving

All to Brothers and
Sisters Divided Equally

Nieces and Nephews to
take their deceased
parent's share.
Half Blood and Whole
Take Equally

FIGURE 6-2

Last Will and Testament
of

I,_____, of the City of _____, County of
_____, State of _____, being of full age and of
sound mind and memory, do make, publish and declare this to be
my last will and testament, hereby revoking all Wills by me
heretofore made.

ITEM I

I direct that my executrix pay all of my funeral expenses, all
enforceable debts, and all succession, legacy, inheritance, death,
transfer, or estate taxes, including any interest and penalties thereon
imposed by any law upon property passing under this Will or
otherwise, testamentary or non-testamentary, out of my residuary
estate as an expense of administration without any apportionment
thereof or reimbursement from any beneficiary.

ITEM II

All the rest of the property, real and personal, of every kind and
description, wheresoever situate, which I may own or have the right
to dispose of at the time of my decease, I give, bequeath and devise
to my wife, _____, absolutely and in fee simple.

ITEM III

In the event that my wife, _____, shall not survive me,
or is considered under the law as not having survived me, then all the
interest in and share of my estate hereinbefore devised and
bequeathed to my said wife shall, by way of substitution, pass to
and vest in my children, _____, and _____,
and any other children who may survive me, equally share and share
alike.

ITEM IV

In the event that any of my children shall have predeceased me
leaving issue surviving them, then such issue shall collectively take
the share which their deceased parent would have taken if living, but
only by right of representation and per stirpes and not per capita.

In the event that any of my children shall predecease me without
leaving issue surviving them, then I direct that their share shall pass
in equal shares to the survivors or all to any one lone survivor.

ITEM V

The provisions made in this Will, unless otherwise specifically provided, are intended to and shall include and relate to all children of mine whether natural born or adopted, and shall include any now living or hereafter born either before or after my decease.

ITEM VI

I make, nominate and appoint my wife,_____, to be the executrix of this, my last will and testament, hereby authorizing and empowering my said executrix to compound, compromise, settle and adjust all claims and demands in favor of or against my estate; to make distribution in cash or in kind; and to sell, at private or public sale, at such prices, and upon such terms of credit or otherwise, as she may deem best, the whole or any part of my real or personal property, and to execute, acknowledge and deliver deeds and other proper instruments of conveyance thereof to the purchaser or purchasers. No purchaser from my executrix need see to the application of the purchase money to or for the purposes of the trust, but the receipt of my executrix shall be a complete discharge and acquittance therefor. I request that no bond be required of my said executrix.

IN WITNESS WHEREOF, I have hereunto set my hand at _____, _____, this_____ day of _____, 19_____.

_____

On the above written date the said_____ declared to us, the undersigned, that the foregoing instrument is his Last Will and Testament, and he requested us to act as witnesses to the same and to his signature thereon, he thereupon signed said Will in our presence, we being present at the same time, and we now at his request and in his presence, and in the presence of each other, do hereunto subscribe our names as witnesses, and we each of us declare that we believe this testator to be of sound mind and memory.

_____residing at_____

_____

_____residing at_____

_____

On occasion a testator may fear a will contest after his death among his heirs, and a no-contest clause is incorporated in the Will. Following is a sample clause.

FIGURE 6-3

```
    If any person shall directly or indirectly resist the

Probate of this Will or contest its validity or maintain before

any judicial body that this is not my last will and testament,

then such person so disputing or contesting my Will shall

forfeit all interest in my estate hereunder and the legacy

herein given to him or her shall be deemed lapsed.
```

At times a testator may wish to devise his real estate to one person, but reserving the right for another person to live in the real estate until his or her death. The interest of the person who holds the property until death is called a life estate, and the interest of the person who receives the property on the death of the other, is the remainder interest. Following is a sample clause which may be inserted in a will to cover this situation.

FIGURE 6-4

```
    I give and devise any interest I may have in any

real estate to my wife, _____, for and during the

term of her natural life with remainder to my step-daughter,

_____, or, in the event she shall not survive my wife,

to her children, equally share and share alike on a per

stirpes and not per capita basis.
```

On occasion a testator may wish to appoint a contingent executor to act in the event of the disability of the first-named executor. A sample clause covering this situation follows.

FIGURE 6-5

```
        I make, nominate and appoint my wife, _____,
to be the executrix of this, my last will and testament,
to serve without bond, but if she predeceases me, dies,
resigns, or is otherwise unable or unwilling to serve as my
executrix, then I make, nominate and appoint my son,
_____, to be my executor, to serve without bond, hereby
authorizing and empowering my said executrix or executor to
compound, compromise, settle and adjust all claims and
demands in favor of or against my estate; to make distributions
in cash or in kind; and to sell, at private or public sale,
at such prices, and upon such terms of credit or otherwise,
as she or he may deem best, the whole or any part of my real
or personal property, and to execute, acknowledge and deliver
deeds and other proper instruments of conveyance thereof
to the purchaser or purchasers.  No purchaser from my
executrix or executor need see to the application of the
purchase money to or for the purposes of the trust, but the
receipt of my executrix or executor shall be a complete
discharge and acquittance therefor.
```

THE CODICIL

Many times a testator wishes to make one small change in his Will. It is not necessary to execute a new will, but a codicil may be made incorporating the change. (See sample codicil.)

FIGURE 6-6

CODICIL

I, _____, of the City of _____,
County of _____, and State of _____, being of
sound mind and memory and not under any restraint, having
made my last will and testament on _____,
do now make, publish, and declare this as and for a codicil
to my said last will and testament as follows:

I revoke Items III and IV of my said last will and
testament and substitute therefor the following Items
III and IV as if originally written in my said last will
and testament as follows:

ITEM III. All the rest and residue of my property,
both real and personal, of every kind and description,
wheresoever situate, which I may own or have the right to
dispose of at the time of my decease, I give, bequeath,
and devise to my daughter, _____; my granddaughter,
_____; and my grandson, _____, and
any other grandchildren who may survive me, equally share
and share alike, absolutely and in fee simple on a per
stirpes basis.

ITEM IV. In the event that neither my daughter or
any grandchildren shall survive me, then I direct that
my estate shall pass as set forth in Item IV of my Last
Will and Testament dated _____.

In all other respects, I hereby ratify and confirm my
said last will and testament.

In Witness Whereof, I hereunto set my hand at _____,
_____, this ____day of _____, 19____, in the
presence of the undersigned witnesses.

_____

Signed, published and declared by the testatrix,
_____, as and for a codicil to her last will and
testament, in our presence, who, at her request, in her
presence, and in the presence of each other, have hereunto
subscribed our names as witnesses at the time and place
aforesaid.

_____residing at _____

_____

_____residing at _____

_____

TRUSTS: TESTAMENTARY AND INTER-VIVOS

A testamentary trust is created by the last will and testament and does not go into effect until the death of the testator or testatrix. An inter-vivos or living trust as it is sometimes known is created by a separate instrument known as a Trust Agreement and is usually made in conjunction with a pour-over will (everything is poured over into the trust).

FIGURE 6-7

Pour-Over Will

LAST WILL AND TESTAMENT
OF
JAMES O. SMITH

I, James O. Smith, of Franklin County, Ohio, do hereby make, publish, and declare this to be my last will and testament, hereby revoking any and all Wills and Codicils by me heretofore made.

ITEM I

I direct that my executrix pay all of my funeral expenses, and all enforceable debts as soon as possible after my death. I direct that all estate, inheritance, succession, legacy and other similar taxes and every part thereof (including interest and penalties thereon) assessed upon or with respect to any property, whether a part of my testamentary estate or not, as a consequence of my death, shall be paid out of my residuary estate as an expense of administration and a general charge against my estate.

ITEM II

I give and bequeath the smaller automobile which I may own at the time of my death to Veronica Smalls, if she should survive me. In the event she should not survive me, I direct that this bequest shall fail and become part of my residuary estate.

I give and bequeath Fifteen Thousand Dollars ($15,000.00) to Veronica Smalls, if she shall survive me. In the event she should not survive me, I direct that this bequest shall fail and become part of my residuary estate.

ITEM III

All the rest and residue of the property, real and personal, of every kind and description, wheresoever situate, including any legacies which may lapse, which I may own or have the right to dispose of at the time of my decease, I give, bequeath and devise to Emily Breckinridge and William Breckinridge, or their successor, as trustee, to be held and disposed of under the trust as provided in the trust agreement entered into between me and said trustees under date of December 1, 1971, at 10:45 o'clock a.m., prior to my signing this Will and as amended at any time prior or subsequent to the execution of this Will. My intention is simply to identify said Trust Agreement and not to incorporate it by reference into this Will or to create a testamentary trust hereby. However, if for any reason said living trust shall not be in existence at the time of my death, or, if for any reason a court or courts of competent jurisdiction shall validly and definitively declare this bequest and devise to be ineffective and invalid, then I give, devise and bequeath all of the said property passing under this paragraph of my Will to Emily Breckinridge and William Breckinridge, or their successors, as trustee, to serve without bond, to be held, managed and distributed in exactly the same manner described in said living trust agreement hereinbefore referred to which, under such circumstances, I do hereby incorporate by reference into this Will to be administered as a testamentary trust.

ITEM IV

I make, nominate and appoint Emily Breckinridge and William Breckinridge to be co-executors of this, my last will and testament, to serve without bond, but if either shall be unable or unwilling to act in this capacity, the other shall act as sole executor, and in the event neither shall be able or willing to act, I make, nominate and appoint the Hunt National Bank to be my executor, to serve without bond, hereby authorizing and empowering my said executrix or executor to compound, compromise, settle and adjust all claims and demands in favor of or against my estate, and to sell, at private or public sale, at such prices, and upon such terms of credit or otherwise, as he or she or it may deem best, the whole or any part of my real or personal property, and to execute, acknowledge and deliver deeds and other proper instruments of conveyance thereof to the purchaser or purchasers. No purchaser from my executrix or executor need see to the application of the purchase money to or for the purposes of the trust, but the receipt of my executrix or executor shall be a complete discharge and acquittance therefor.

My executrix or executor is authorized and empowered, without court order or other legal formality and without compliance with Section 2113.30 of the Revised Code of Ohio, or any other law of similar import, to hold, retain and continue to operate solely at the risk of my estate any business enterprise that I may own in whole or in part at the time of my death, whether a sole proprietorship, partnership, or corporation; to employ such managers, employees, or agents, as she, he or it deems advisable in the management of said business, and to do and perform all other acts which my executrix or executor, in her, his or its sole and absolute discretion, may deem necessary and advisable in the operation of such business; and to dissolve, liquidate, or sell such business at such time and upon such terms as my executrix or executor in her, his or its sole and absolute discretion, deems for the best interest of my estate.

IN WITNESS WHEREOF, I have hereunto set my hand at Columbus, Ohio, this_____ day of _____, 19__.

_____
                                    James O. Smith

On the above written date the said James O. Smith declared to us, the undersigned, that the foregoing instrument is his Last Will and Testament, and he requested us to act as witnesses to the same and to his signature thereon, he thereupon signed said Will in our presence, we being present at the same time, and we now at his request and in his presence, and in the presence of each other, do hereunto subscribe our names as witnesses, and we each of us declare that we believe this testator to be of sound mind and memory.

_____residing at_____

_____

_____residing at_____

_____

This type of trust goes into effect during the lifetime of the grantor. Inter-vivos trusts may be revocable or irrevocable. Both types of trusts are created to make financial provisions for a spouse, children, grandchildren, parent, or whomever the testator or grantor wishes to provide for.

Rule Against Perpetuity. Trusts may not go on indefinitely. Following is a clause known as the "Rule Against Perpetuity Clause" which may be inserted in a trust will to comply with the rule.

FIGURE 6-8

(Rule Against Perpetuity Clause)

```
     ITEM EIGHT: Anything to the contrary notwithstanding,
the trusts created herein shall terminate not later than
twenty-one (21) years after the death of the last survivor
of the group composed of myself, my wife and my children,
and if any trust created herein has not sooner terminated,
the Trustee at said time shall pay over, convey and
deliver the remaining trust assets then in its possession
in equal shares to the persons then entitled to receive
the income therefrom.
```

Spendthrift Clause. To prevent beneficiaries of a trust from carelessly depleting the assets of the trust, sometimes a clause known as the "Spendthrift" clause is inserted in a trust. Following is an example.

FIGURE 6-9

Spendthrift Clause

ITEM SEVEN: The income and principal of the trusts herein created shall not be alienated or disposed of, or in any manner encumbered by the beneficiaries thereof while in the possession and control of the Trustee. If a beneficiary shall alienate, charge or dispose of his or her said income or principal, or any part thereof, or any interest therein, or if by reason of his or her bankruptcy, or other event at any time happening during the continuance of this trust, said income or principal otherwise intended for said beneficiary shall wholly or in part cease to be enjoyed by him or her as above provided. In such event, the trust hereinbefore expressed concerning said income and principal shall thereupon cease and terminate as to such beneficiary, and, all income and principal otherwise hereinbefore provided for him or her shall thereafter be held and distributed by the Trustee for him or her, during the remainder of his or her life, according to the absolute discretion of the Trustee. But the Trustee may, nevertheless, pay to him or her or for his or her health, maintenance, support and education, or to his or her child, children, or spouse thereafter, from such income and principal, such sums as it, in its absolute discretion, shall think fit and proper having regard for my wishes as in this Last Will and Testament expressed, and retaining any unexpended sums as part of the principal of the trust to be finally disposed of after the death of such beneficiary as herein provided.

Powers of the Trustee are usually spelled out in great detail. Following is a sample of the usual powers granted to a trustee.

FIGURE 6-10

Powers of the Trustee

ITEM NINE: My Trustee shall serve without bond and shall have full power without any order of court therefor:

(a) to hold and retain any of the property coming into its possession hereunder (including shares stock of Bank _____ Corporation) in the same form of investment as those forms in which it was received by said Trustee, even though such retention may result in a disproportionate concentration in one class of property, without incurring liability in any way for any loss of principal or income caused by the decline in value of any such investment or investments;

(b) to sell at public or private sale, exchange, lease for any period of time, whether longer or shorter than the duration of this trust, borrow money and mortgage or pledge any property, real or personal, at any time constituting a portion of said trust upon such terms and conditions as said Trustee shall deem wise;

(c) to invest and reinvest any money, whether income or principal, at any time in said trust in such bonds, stocks, notes, real estate mortgages or other securities, life insurance or in such other property, real or personal, or in a common trust fund as said Trustee shall deem wise without being limited by any statute or rule of law of the State of Ohio regarding investments by Trustees now or hereafter in effect;

(d) to cause any security or other property which may at any time constitute a portion of said trust to be issued, held or registered in the name of a nominee or in such form that title will pass by delivery;

(e) to vote by proxy or in person and exercise all other rights in relation to all stocks and securities contained in said trust;

(f) to enter into option or voting trust agreements and to consent to the liquidation, reorganization, consolidation, readjustment of the financial structure or sale of the assets of any corporation or other organization, the securities of which constitute a portion of said trust and to take any action with reference to such securities which in the opinion of the Trustee is necessary to obtain the benefit of any such reorganization, consolidation, readjustment or sale; to exercise any conversion privilege or subscription right given to it as the owner of any security constituting a portion of said trust; to accept and hold as a portion of said trust the securities resulting from any such reorganization, consolidation, readjustment, sale, conversion or subscription;

(g) to hold, administer, maintain and manage any real estate coming into the trust estate paying all taxes, assessments, maintenance and other proper charges thereon, with full power to mortgage the said real estate if necessary for the purposes of conserving the said trust estate; and to make such improvements, additions and/or alterations as in its judgment will be beneficial to said real estate and to charge the costs and expenses thereof to principal and/or income as the Trustee shall deem equitable;

(h) to make any distribution of said trust in cash or in kind, or partly in cash and partly in kind, at such valuations as said Trustee, in its absolute and uncontrolled discretion, shall deem proper and equitable, and such decision of the Trustee shall be final and binding upon all beneficiaries hereunder;

(i) to make payments to a minor beneficiary, or to the person with whom such minor is living, without requiring the appointment of a legal guardian to receive such payments, and the receipt signed by such minor beneficiary, or his or her natural guardian, or the person with whom such minor is living, shall discharge the Trustee of any liability to see to the application of such payment;

(j) to continue, liquidate or incorporate any business in which I may be engaged without liability for any losses;

(k) to determine what is income and what is principal, and to charge or credit expenses, gains, losses, premiums, discounts, waste and appreciation or depreciation in value to principal or income, or partly to each, as it may deem just. The foregoing power shall apply to, but not be limited to, cash and noncash dividends, stock dividends, liquidating dividends, premiums and discounts on the purchase of investments, and includes the power to set up or not to set up reserves and sinking funds for taxes, assessments, insurance premiums, repairs, improvements, depreciation, obsolescense and maintenance, and for any other purposes;

(l) to employ such attorneys, agents and consultants as it may deem necessary in the administration of this trust, and to pay to them from this trust reasonable compensation for services rendered by them.

Trust Wills and Trust Agreements can be quite lengthy, running to fifteen or more pages in length. The attorney may keep sample trust wills and trust agreements on hand from which to dictate and from which you may copy certain standard clauses and powers given to the trustee.

SAFE DEPOSIT BOX

Many attorneys maintain large safe deposit boxes in banks and hold in them original, executed wills of their clients for safekeeping and other valuables, such as jewelry, valuable coins, Series E bonds, stock certificates, etc. being held for an estate. It may be expedient for you to be authorized as a deputy for the box so that you may enter it from time to time to place valuable documents and remove them for the attorney. Keep wills placed in the safe deposit box in alphabetical order for quick retrieval.

CONTROL RECORDS FOR THE SAFE DEPOSIT BOX

The safe deposit box containing many clients' wills and valuables of estates could become a useless file if there were no records kept. It would necessitate going to the bank to ascertain if a certain item were in the box. To avoid this, maintain a small 3x5 card file with an alphabetical set of indexes. Each time an item is placed in the box, make up a 3x5 card for the client or estate, last name typed first. If the client already has an item in the box add it to a previous card; each client should have only one card. List the item on the card with the date deposited.

FIGURE 6-11

File Card for the Safe Deposit Box

```
Kirtzinger, Helen

11-1-71        Will dated 1-1-71
11-1-71        Certificate of Deposit
                 State Bank $10,000
```

To avoid a bulky file, remove the cards when the client's valuables have all been removed from the box. Make a notation on the card as to the date of removal of the item and to whom it was given. Retain these cards, however, in another place as the attorney may wish to know at some future date when the valuable or document was removed and to whom it was given.

Guardianships

When the attorney handles guardianships, you may take over after the initial guardianship is set up by the attorney, and the income and expenses are determined.

RECEIVING AND DISBURSING FUNDS

Once the income has been determined and the bank account has been set up with the bank, you may receive all funds and deposit them as they are received, keeping an accurate record of the monies received, and what they represent. The income, for example, may consist of Social Security, Veterans' Administration, retirement pensions, or annuities from life insurance companies, etc. Keep a record of the date of each check deposited in the account.

The ward may be living in a nursing home, a county home, or may be maintaining a home of his own for which the guardian must pay all expenses. As the bills are received, pay them, keeping a record of the payments and what they are for. Keep a careful balance on the account sheet so that the account will not be overdrawn. If the monthly income exceeds the monthly disbursements, a savings account may be set up in a savings and loan institution for the excess in the name of the guardian. This may be drawn on for emergencies and unusual expenses of the ward.

Once a month the account sheet should be reconciled with the bank statement.

FIGURE 6-12

Guardianship Account Sheet

		Receipts	Disbursement	Balance
19__				
8-30	Veterans Administration	$1,125.00		
31	Mrs. Burns		25.00	
9- 3	Clarendon Hotel for ward		307.19	
13	Mrs. Burns		25.00	
13	Veterans Administration	375.00		
	Clarendon Hotel		117.05	
	Brandon Hotel 4-23 thru 8-16		270.20	
	Brandon Hotel to 10-1		37.50	
19	Mrs. Burns		30.00	
28	Probate Court costs		10.50	
	Brown Ins. Agency, bond		26.25	
	Homer J. Black, reimbursement for mileage to take ward to VA Hosp.		10.90	
	Townsend Veterinarian for dog		52.50	
30	Mrs. Burns		50.00	
	Ohio Dept. of Health, birth certificate for ward		1.00	
	VA Hospital, Incidentals for ward for Sept. & Oct.		60.00	
	VA Hospital, clothing for ward		79.85	
	Bank charges		.62	
30	Balance reconciled with bank			396.94

Note: An accountant's ruled, columnar work sheet may be used.

PREPARING THE GUARDIAN'S ACCOUNT

The Veterans Administration and Social Security Administration require that an accounting be filed once a year. Guardianships receiving other funds may file accountings according to the requirements of their state codes (sometimes every two years).

FIGURE 6-13

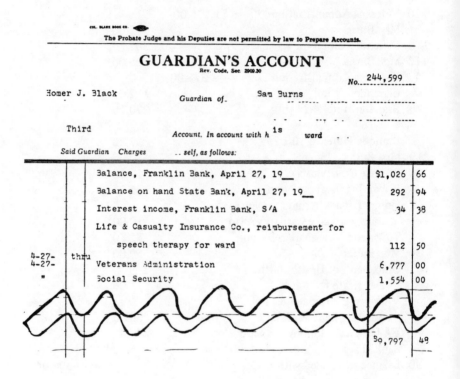

Since you keep all records of income and disbursements, you may prepare the accounting. Usually a form for this is provided by the local Probate Court. It consists of a listing of all income during the accounting period covered and all disbursements. It also shows a recapitulation which includes the balance due the estate. The balance due the estate should reconcile with the balance in the checking account and savings account, if any. Number each disbursement and

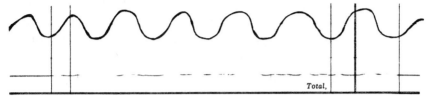

Total,

RECAPITULATION

give the corresponding cancelled check the same number. The account must also list all investments made under the guardianship. The account then concludes with an affidavit by the guardian that the account is true and accurate, which you may notarize. The attorney then files the accounting with the Probate Court.

_____
                                                    Guardian

AFFIDAVIT
_____

The State of Ohio, Franklin County, ss.

I, _____ *Guardian of* _____

_____

do make solemn oath that the within is a full, true and correct account of my said Guardianship as I

verily believe.

_____
                            ADDRESS

Sworn to before me and signed in my presence, this _____ *day of* _____ , 19 ____

_____

Estates

In the processing of estates you also may become a right arm to the attorney. Procedures are fairly routine and once you become thoroughly familiar with them you and the attorney will find that with just a few words of instruction and direction and a minimum of dictation you can proceed to fill out the necessary forms to admit a will to probate, appoint an executor or administrator, prepare a waiver of notice, transfer or sell personal property, transfer real estate, and, if you are an advanced secretary, you may even prepare state estate tax papers, Federal estate tax returns, fiduciary returns, and final and distributive accounts.

There are special actions in Probate work such as an action to determine heirship (when the deceased is intestate), estates involving the "half and half" statute, and actions to sell real estate, which must be dictated by the attorney, but whether advanced or not your role in preparing estate matters should be one of great care in your typing and preparation so that the papers will be neat and accurate. These matters are perpetuated through abstracts, often being incorporated in them. Careful preparation by you also speaks well for the attorney and gives him a reputation, not only with his clients, but with the other officers of the court.

INTERVIEW WITH DECEASED'S RELATIVES

Usually the attorney conducts the initial interview with the deceased person's relatives as the attorney-client relationship is important and, in addition, there are judgments and decisions to be made by the attorney regarding the best way to conduct the administration of the estate.

However, should your attorney permit you to interview initially, following is a sample interview sheet which calls for the basic information that would be needed.

FIGURE 6-14

Interview Sheet

Name of deceased_____

Date of death_____Date of birth_____Causes of death____
_____

Deceased's residence_____

Deceased's Social Security number_____Occupation_____

Was there a Will? Yes_____ No_____Bond waived?_____

Executor's name_____

        address_____

        telephone number_____

Next of Kin:

Name	Relation- ship	Address	Age
_____	_____	_____	_____
_____	_____	_____	_____
_____	_____	_____	_____
_____	_____	_____	_____
_____	_____	_____	_____
_____	_____	_____	_____
_____	_____	_____	_____
_____	_____	_____	_____
_____	_____	_____	_____
_____	_____	_____	_____

Bank accounts:

Bank	Account number	Savings or Checking
_____	_____	_____
_____	_____	_____
_____	_____	_____

Auto:

Make	Year	Model	Serial	Certificate of Title No.
_____	_____	_____	_____	_____
_____	_____	_____	_____	_____

Stocks or bonds:

Serial No.	Company	No. of Shares or face amount
_____	_____	_____
_____	_____	_____
_____	_____	_____
_____	_____	_____

REAL ESTATE:

Address of property_____

Fee holder_____

Legal description:

Household Goods and Furnishings:

Jewelry:

Accounts Receivable:

Debtor	Kind of claim	Amount
_____	_____	_____
_____	_____	_____
_____	_____	_____
_____	_____	_____

Joint and Survivorship Property:

_____

_____

_____

_____

Insurance Contracts:

Company	Face Amount	Policy No.
_____	_____	_____
_____	_____	_____
_____	_____	_____

Debts of decedent:

Creditor	Address	Amount
_____	_____	_____
_____	_____	_____
_____	_____	_____
_____	_____	_____

Documents left with attorney:

Insurance policies:

_____

Abstract_____

Passbooks_____

Stocks and bonds_____

Auto title_____

Other_____

RECEIVING AND DISBURSING FUNDS

Often the law office will receive and disburse all funds in an estate with the executor or administrator authorized to sign the checks, and sometimes co-signing with the attorney. This is the best method since it is a simple matter in this case for you or the attorney to make up an account if the records are kept in the law office. When the fiduciary keeps the checkbook and receives and disburses the funds outside the law office, it is necessary to request all cancelled checks and bank statements from him before an accounting can be made.

The account records for receipts and disbursements can be kept in the same manner as for guardianships (explained at the beginning of this chapter). In addition, it is well to maintain the record date of stock dividend checks. This date is either given on the check or enclosed with it.

The bank statement should be reconciled once a month.

TIMELY FILINGS

Each state has its own requirements for filing estate matters. It is important that timely filings be made and that the estate not be unnecessarily dragged out. Of course, this is the attorney's responsibility, but you may set up a reminder system to help your attorney file on time. A diary system may be used. When a new estate is opened, note in your diary thirty days from date of appointment (for example) that the inventory is due. You might be called upon to contact the appraisers and arrange a time convenient to all to appraise the real estate. You can then proceed in the same manner to diary the entire estate, such as Schedule of Debts, State Estate tax application, Federal estate tax return, if required, accounts, etc.

FIGURE 6-15

Time Schedule for Estates
State of Ohio

1 month—after appointment of executor or administrator—file INVENTORY AND APPRAISEMENT and Preliminary Notice of Ohio Estate Tax

2 months—after appointment of fiduciary—FEDERAL ESTATE TAX PRELIMINARY NOTICE, if over $60,000

4 months and within 5 months of appointment—SCHEDULE OF DEBTS (Claims against the estate must be filed within four months of the date of appointment, but a claim may be filed after this four-month period by filing a petition with the Court to present the claim. However, a claim not presented within nine months of the date of appointment is forever barred.)

1 year—Ohio Estate Tax must be filed within one year. It may be paid any time after 6 months and a discount of 1% per month is given if it is paid prior to the one-year time limit.

15 months—Federal Estate Tax must be filed within 15 months from the date of death.

Distribution may be made six months from the date of appointment if there are no debts outstanding against the estate and there are no suits filed against the estate.

First account is due 9 months from the date of appointment. This may also be a Final Account if all the debts and Taxes have been paid and the distribution is completed.

THE SCHEDULE OF DEBTS

By the time the schedule of debts is due the attorney usually will have gathered together all of the decedent's debts, or if the interview sheet is used, the debts will be available to make up the Schedule of Debts.

Classification of Debts. Debts are paid according to a definite priority set by the state code. Each debt is classified accordingly. Keep handy a list of the classifications as set by your state code typed on an 8½x11 sheet of bond and placed in a sheet protector so that you may aid the attorney in classifying debts.

FIGURE 6-16

CLASSIFICATION OF DEBTS
State of Ohio

A. Costs and expenses of administration.

B. Bill of funeral director not exceeding five hundred dollars and such funeral expenses other than the bill of the funeral director as are approved by the probate court.

C. The allowance made to the widow and children for their support for twelve months.

D. Debts entitled to a preference under the laws of the United States.

E. Expenses of the last sickness of the decedent.

F. Personal property taxes and obligations for which the decedent was personally liable to the state or any subdivision thereof.

G. Debts for manual labor performed for the deceased within twelve months preceding decedent's death, not exceeding one hundred fifty dollars to any one person.

H. Other debts as to which claims have been presented within four months after the appointment of the executor or administrator.

I. All other debts for which claims have been presented after four months from the appointment of the executor or administrator.

Such part of the bill of the funeral director as exceeds five hundred dollars and such part of a claim included in division G of this section as exceeds one hundred fifty dollars shall be included as a debt under division H or I of this section, depending upon the time when the claim for such additional amount is presented. This section does not repeal or modify Section 5105.13 of the Revised Code.

PREPARING THE ACCOUNT

Some large estates are held open long enough to require a first, second or third account before the final and distributive account is filed. If the account records are maintained as described above, the first account (or the first, final and distributive) may be easily made from the account sheet.

If the account sheet is reconciled monthly with the bank statement, the account should be in balance at all times. The receipts may be listed either daily or sometimes lumped together for convenience and to shorten the account. For example, the estate might have received monthly payments of $100 for rental of real estate. Instead of listing each payment the income could be listed as follows:

Rental of Real Estate, 12 payments @ $100 $1,200.00

The disbursements may be listed the same way, either individually or lumped together.

If the account is a first account, the balance due the estate should equal the balance in the checking account as of the end of the accounting period.

The list of securities involved in the estate should show each security.

If the account is final and distributive the account should show disbursement of every item that was listed in the inventory; each debt listed on the Schedule of Debts must have been paid and listed in the final account; and each bequest under the will must be shown.

Number each item of disbursement on the account, and give the corresponding cancelled check the same number. The checks then serve as receipts for the disbursements.

In preparing the account, first prepare a handwritten draft on a legal pad and make certain the account is in balance before typing it.

ADVANCEMENT OF CASH BY SPOUSE TO AVOID SALE OF
REAL ESTATE TO PAY DEBTS

Often in a small estate the deceased had nothing but his residence. There are debts to pay and, rather than sell the real estate to pay them, the surviving spouse will pay the debts. The final account will show this as income into the estate as follows:

Advanced by Nancy M. Martin to avoid sale of real estate to pay
debts $3,000.00

Adoptions

Many times adoptions are handled through agencies and the
adoptive parents are not to be told the infant's name or its parents'
names. Exercise extreme care in this type adoption that you not
reveal this information to the adoptive parents. If you prepare papers
to be signed by the adoptive parents, and they come into the office
to sign the papers, the paper should be covered except for the
signature line, lest information be revealed.

On occasion you may be called upon to go to the hospital with the
attorney to pick up the newborn infant and deliver it to the adoptive
parents. Usually the adoptive parents will send along the necessary
clothing for the nurse to dress the infant in before it leaves the
hospital.

In the case of adoptions arranged before the infant is born, the
adopting parents will often agree to pay all hospital and medical bills
for the expectant mother.

In the case of a mother with a child remarrying and the new
husband wishing to adopt the child, the attorney may ask the blood
father to sign a consent. Following is a sample consent.

FIGURE 6-17

IN THE PROBATE COURT OF FRANKLIN COUNTY, OHIO

IN THE MATTER OF THE ADOPTION OF: NO._____

CONSENT TO ADOPT

The undersigned, _____, represents that he is qualified to consent to the adoption of _____, as provided in Ohio Revised Code 3107.07, by virtue of being the natural father of the child, and he hereby waives notice of the hearing on the petition filed in said court on the _____day of _____, 19____, and hereby consents to the adoption of said child proposed by said petitioner.

I further waive notice of any investigation made, reports admitted, or availability for examination of the contents of any report hereafter submitted by the next friend appointed by the court in the case.

_____
(name of father)

STATE OF

COUNTY OF   , SS:

_____(father), being first duly cautioned and sworn, says that the facts stated and the allegations made in the foregoing consent are true as he verily believes.

_____
(name of father)

Sworn to before me and subscribed in my presence this _____day of _____, 19____.

_____
Notary Public

DECREES

There are two types of decrees given in an adoption matter. In some cases an interlocutory or temporary decree is granted. At a later date a final decree is granted. In some cases the final decree is given at the end of the required waiting period.

FIGURE 6-18

IN THE PROBATE COURT OF FRANKLIN COUNTY, OHIO
IN THE MATTER OF THE ADOPTION
OF_____   No._____

Interlocutory Order of Adoption

This day this cause came on for a full hearing upon the petition of_____ and_____ for the adoption and change of name of an infant_____(name), the necessary answer and consent, the report of the next friend of the child, and the evidence.

It appearing to the Court that lawful notice of the time and place of this hearing has been given to all persons entitled to notice or that they have entered their appearance herein, the Court finds that all the necessary parties are before the Court.

Whereupon the Court, having examined under oath, the petitioners separately and apart from each other, the next friend of said child, and all persons in interest who were present, finds that each of the petitioners of his or her own free will and accord desires said adoption and that they are husband and wife, and that the child has been in the home of the petitioners since_____

The Court further finds from the testimony in evidence that the petitioners are suitably qualified to care for and rear said child, and that the best interests of the child will be promoted at Columbus, Ohio, and that there has been a compliance with the provisions of the adoption code.

The Court further finds that the child was legally placed in the home of the petitioners, and that said placement was beneficial to the child.

It is, therefore, ORDERED by the Court that an interlocutory decree of adoption, be and the same is hereby entered, declaring that from this date and henceforth, subject to the final decree of the Court to be entered at a time not less than six (6) months from this date, said child shall have the status of the adopted child of said petitioners, and the name of said child shall be changed to _____, provided, however, that property rights shall not be affected by this interlocutory order; and this cause is continued.

_____
Probate Judge

Approved:

_____
Attorney for Petitioners

FIGURE 6-19

IN THE PROBATE COURT OF FRANKLIN COUNTY, OHIO

IN THE MATTER OF THE ADOPTION OF

_____   No._____

Final Decree of Adoption

This day this cause came on for a final hearing before the Court upon the petition of_____ and_____ and the proceedings had thereafter, for the adoption of_____, who, prior to the interlocutory decree entered herein, was known as infant_____, and who was born on the_____ day of _____, _____, at _____, _____, _____County.

It appearing to the Court that more than six months have expired from the date on which the Court entered the interlocutory decree of adoption herein, and that said interlocutory decree has not been revoked, and it further appearing that the next friend heretofore appointed by the Court has submitted to the Court a further report of their findings, relative to the suitability of this adoption, the Court finds that said adoption will be to the best interests of said child.

It is, therefore, ORDERED AND ADJUDGED by the Court that a final decree of adoption be and is hereby entered in this adoption, and that henceforth said child shall have the status of an adopted child of said petitioners.

_____
                                                    Probate Judge

Approved:

_____
Attorney for Petitioners

OBTAINING A NEW BIRTH CERTIFICATE

Some states have provided by statute that the birth certificate of an adopted child must read as though it were the original. In these states the new birth certificate may be applied for after adoption proceedings have become final. The adoptive parents should be listed as the parents when making the application.

Miscellaneous Forms

STATUTORY EXECUTOR'S DEED

If your state authorizes a statutory short form executor's deed, it can save much typing time. Following is an example.

FIGURE 6-20

EXECUTOR'S DEED
(Statutory Form - Ohio Revised Code No. 5301)

_____, Executor of the Will of
_____, deceased, by power conferred by
the Probate Court of Franklin County, Ohio, in Case No.
_____, and by the statutes of the State of Ohio and
every other power, in consideration of One Dollar ($1.00)
and other good and valuable consideration, receipt of which
is hereby acknowledged, grants with fiduciary covenants and
general warranty covenants to _____ and _____,
whose tax mailing address is _____,
the following real property:

          (Here describe property)

    Last Transfer: Deed Book_____, Page _____.

    Subject to easements, conditions and restrictions of
record, if any, and taxes and assessments, if any, not yet
due and payable.

    WITNESS My Hand this ____day of _____, 19__.

Signed in the presence of:

_____

               Executor of the Estate of

_____

STATE OF OHIO
COUNTY OF FRANKLIN, SS:

    Before me, a Notary Public in and for said County,
personally appeared _____, Executor of the Estate of
_____, deceased, and acknowledged his signing
of the foregoing deed to be his voluntary act and deed as such
Executor, for the purposes therein mentioned.

    IN WITNESS WHEREOF, I have hereunto set my hand and
affixed my official seal at _____, this ____day
of _____, 19__.

                           _____
                              Notary Public

Prepared by: (Attorney's name and address)

Following are a few miscellaneous forms of pleadings that cover various types of matters that might arise in Probate work. If you keep this type form in your form book you can prepare the necessary pleadings without dictation, when instructed to do so by the attorney.

After the attorney has established an individual function, and it becomes repetitive, you may take over the function and see that it is performed regularly.

FIGURE 6-21

Agreement Releasing Administrator from Liability
When Making Distribution

AGREEMENT

WHEREAS, ⎯⎯⎯⎯⎯⎯⎯⎯, acting as administrator of the estate of ⎯⎯⎯⎯⎯⎯⎯, ⎯⎯⎯⎯⎯⎯⎯ County Probate Court No.⎯⎯⎯⎯⎯⎯, and

WHEREAS, the undersigned ⎯⎯⎯⎯⎯⎯⎯⎯⎯⎯, and ⎯⎯⎯⎯⎯⎯⎯ desire distribution in full from said estate of their distributive shares, and

WHEREAS, final release from the United States Internal Revenue Service, and the State of Ohio, with regard to Federal Income Taxes, Federal Estate Taxes, and Personal Property Taxes has not been obtained;

NOW, THEREFORE, in consideration of⎯⎯⎯⎯⎯⎯⎯⎯⎯⎯
                                                                    (administrator)

making distribution to the undersigned in full of the assets remaining in the Estate of⎯⎯⎯⎯⎯⎯⎯, the undersigned do hereby agree and bind themselves, their heirs, executors and assigns to reimburse said ⎯⎯⎯⎯⎯⎯⎯(administrator) for any amount which he may be required to pay as a result of any possible assessments made with regard to the above tax matters.

Signed at⎯⎯⎯⎯⎯⎯⎯, this ⎯⎯⎯ day of ⎯⎯⎯⎯⎯⎯⎯, 19⎯⎯.

⎯⎯⎯⎯⎯⎯⎯⎯⎯⎯⎯⎯⎯

⎯⎯⎯⎯⎯⎯⎯⎯⎯⎯⎯⎯⎯

FIGURE 6-22

IN THE PROBATE COURT OF FRANKLIN COUNTY, OHIO

IN THE MATTER OF THE ESTATE OF

DECEASED   No._____

APPLICATION FOR AUTHORITY TO PURCHASE MEMORIAL

Now comes _____, Administrator of the
Estate of _____, deceased, and makes
application to the Court for authority to purchase a suitable
memorial for the above-named decedent.

Applicant says that decedent was buried on the family
plot and that a memorial to match the other markers now
on said lot may be purchased from the _____
(name of memorial company) at a total cost of $_____.

WHEREFORE, applicant prays the Court that authority be
granted to purchase a memorial from _____ at a
cost of $_____, and that he be authorized to include the
same in his next accounting herein.

_____
Administrator

STATE OF OHIO
COUNTY OF FRANKLIN, SS:

_____, being first duly sworn, deposes
and says that the facts stated in the foregoing application
are true as he verily believes.

_____
(Administrator's name)

Sworn to before me and subscribed in my presence this
_____day of _____, _____.

_____
Notary Public

FIGURE 6-23

IN THE PROBATE COURT OF FRANKLIN COUNTY, OHIO

IN THE MATTER OF THE ESTATE OF

DECEASED   No. _____

JOURNAL ENTRY GRANTING AUTHORITY TO
PURCHASE MEMORIAL

This cause came on for hearing on application of
_____, Administrator of the Estate of
_____, deceased, for authority to purchase a
memorial for the above-named decedent as set forth in his
application.

The Court upon due consideration hereby authorizes
the application to purchase a memorial from _____
for the sum of $_____, and to include said amount in his
next account.

_____
Probate Judge

Approved:

_____
Attorney

FIGURE 6-24

IN THE PROBATE COURT OF FRANKLIN COUNTY, OHIO

IN THE MATTER OF THE ESTATE OF

DECEASED   NO._____

REPORT OF NEWLY DISCOVERED ASSETS

Now comes _____ as administrator of
the Estate of _____, deceased, and says that
the following is an itemized report of newly discovered
assets which have come into his hands since the filing
of the original inventory. Such assets with an estimate of
the value thereof, are as follows:

Description   Estimated Value

        (List assets)

_____
                Administrator

STATE OF OHIO
COUNTY OF FRANKLIN, SS:

       _____, Administrator, Estate of
_____, being first duly sworn, deposes and
says that the facts stated in the foregoing report are true.

_____
            (Administrator's Name)

     Sworn to before me and subscribed in my presence this
_____day of _____, 19_____.

_____
            Notary Public

FIGURE 6-25

     IN THE PROBATE COURT OF FRANKLIN COUNTY, OHIO

IN THE MATTER OF THE ESTATE OF

DECEASED   No. _____

JOURNAL ENTRY

     This day _____, as administrator of the
Estate of _____, deceased, submitted a report
of newly discovered assets, and the Court being fully
advised in the premises, authorizes the filing of the same
without an inventory or appraisement of such assets.

_____
            Probate Judge

Approved:

_____
Attorney

FIGURE 6-26

```
        IN THE PROBATE COURT OF FRANKLIN COUNTY, OHIO
   IN THE MATTER OF THE ESTATE OF

   DECEASED                              No._____
```

APPLICATION FOR AUTHORITY TO PAY ATTORNEY FEES

Now comes _____, Executor of the Estate of
_____, deceased, and makes application for an
order of the court allowing attorney fees.

Said executor represents that in order to make a proper
administration of the estate, it was necessary for him to
employ an attorney at law, who handled all legal matters
concerning the estate, including Federal income tax matters.

Said executor further represents that the legal
services were beneficial to the estate; are reasonably worth
the sum of $_____; and that said amount is not more than
the amount usually charged for said services in the
community.

WHEREFORE, your applicant prays that the court allow
attorney fees in the sum of $_____; and authorize the
payment of the same out of the assets of said estate.

                                    _____
                                           Executor

STATE OF OHIO,
COUNTY OF FRANKLIN, SS:

_____, being first duly sworn, deposes
and says that the facts stated in the foregoing application
are true as he verily believes.

                                    _____
                                        (Executor's name)

Sworn to before me and subscribed in my presence this
_____day of _____, 19_____.

                                    _____
                                          Notary Public

FIGURE 6-27

IN THE PROBATE COURT OF FRANKLIN COUNTY, OHIO

IN THE MATTER OF THE ESTATE OF

DECEASED   No._____

JOURNAL ENTRY ALLOWING ATTORNEY FEES

This day this cause came on to be heard on the application of _____, Executrix of the Estate of _____ for an allowance of attorney fees.

Whereupon, it appearing to the Court that it was necessary to employ an attorney to make a proper administration of said estate, and that the legal services so rendered are reasonably worth the sum of $_____;

It is, therefore, ORDERED by the Court that said executrix be and she is hereby allowed out of the assets of said estate, the sum of $_____for attorney fees.

_____
Probate Judge

Approved:

_____
Attorney

FIGURE 6-28

IN THE PROBATE COURT OF FRANKLIN COUNTY, OHIO

IN THE MATTER OF THE ESTATE OF

DECEASED   No._____

WAIVER OF NOTICE AND CONSENT TO
PAYMENT OF ATTORNEY FEES

The undersigned, being one of the residuary legatees of the Estate of _____, does hereby waive notice of the time and place and does hereby waive the right to have any hearing on the application for allowance of attorney fees as filed in this estate by _____ (attorney) for services performed for the estate, and does hereby consent to the payment of the sum of $_____ to _____(attorney) for such legal services; and further consents that such payment may be made from the assets of the estate.

Signed at _____, this _____day of _____, 19_____.

_____

FIGURE 6-29

IN THE PROBATE COURT OF FRANKLIN COUNTY, OHIO
IN THE MATTER OF THE ESTATE OF
DECEASED   No._____

Application to Reopen Estate

Now comes_____ and represents to the Court that she
was appointed Executrix of the Estate of said decedent on
_____; that included in the Inventory and Appraisement
filed in said Estate were 15 shares of the common stock of National
Standard Life Insurance Company, Orlando, Florida; that the Application for Determination of the Ohio Inheritance Tax was duly filed
in said estate proceedings and that the above described shares of
stock were included in said Application; that the Ohio Inheritance
Tax was duly determined and paid by said Executrix; that subsequent to the filing of the Inventory and Appraisement and the
determination and payment of the Ohio Inheritance Tax, stock splits
and stock dividends declared on said original 15 shares of common
stock have increased the number of shares to 254 shares, which
shares are registered in the name of_____, Executrix of
the Estate of_____; that said Executrix filed her First,
Final, and Distributive account in said Estate and on_____
said account was confirmed, the Estate settled and the Executrix
discharged.

Your applicant further represents that she is the sole legatee
under the terms of the Last Will and Testament of said decedent;
and that she failed to transfer and distribute to herself as the sole
legatee said 254 shares of the common stock of National Standard
Life Insurance Company, Orlando, Florida; and that by reason of
her discharge by this court as such Executrix, said company now
refuses to transfer said shares on its books; and that it will be
necessary for her to reopen said Estate in order to transfer said
shares and complete the administration of said Estate.

Wherefore, your applicant prays an order of the Court reopening
this Estate for the purpose of effecting the transfer of the above
described shares of stock and any other acts necessary to complete
the administration of this Estate.

_____
Executrix

FIGURE 6-30

IN THE PROBATE COURT OF FRANKLIN COUNTY, OHIO

IN THE MATTER OF THE ESTATE OF

DECEASED   No._____

ENTRY

This cause came on to be heard upon the application of
_____, Executrix of the Estate of _____,
for an order of the Court to reopen the above Estate; the
Court upon consideration, finds that the facts stated and
representations made in said Application are true and that
it is necessary to reopen said Estate for the purpose of
completing the transfer to the legatee of said Estate, of
254 shares of common stock of National Standard Life Insurance
Company, including any impounded cash dividends thereon, and
any other acts required to fully complete the administration
of said Estate.

It is therefore ordered, adjudged and decreed that the
Estate of _____, deceased, be and it hereby is
reopened for the purpose of transferring to the legatee of said
Estate 254 shares of common stock of National Standard Life
Insurance Company, Orlando, Florida, including any impounded
cash dividends thereon; and any other acts required to fully
complete the administration of said Estate.

_____
Probate Judge

Approved:

_____
Attorney

FIGURE 6-31

IN THE PROBATE COURT OF FRANKLIN COUNTY, OHIO

Style of case   No._____

Affidavit for Service by Publication

STATE OF OHIO

COUNTY OF FRANKLIN, SS:

Now comes the plaintiff, being first duly cautioned and sworn
and deposes and states that the residences of the defendants are
unknown and cannot be with reasonable diligence ascertained.

Further affiant states that the defendants' places of residence cannot be ascertained and that the case is one of those mentioned in Section 2703.14 of the Revised Code of Ohio, to-wit: Sub Section (f).

The affiant further states that he is the duly appointed administrator of the Estate of_____, deceased.

Further the affiant deposes and saith not.

_____
Administrator

Sworn to before me and subscribed in my presence this_____ day of_____, 19_____.

_____
Notary Public

SEVEN

You and Domestic Relations Law

The Domestic Relations or Family Law as it is sometimes called embraces the whole area of the family relationship. Many law firms spend as much time trying to effect reconciliations by referring their clients to marriage counselors and psychiatrists as they do in the divorce courts. Some states, notably California, have initiated the no-fault divorce. The sample pleadings which are presented in this chapter comply with the Civil Rules in Ohio and are patterned after the Federal Civil Rules. The brevity of the pleadings is characteristic.

The Interview Sheet

The first step with a divorce client is the interview between the client and the attorney. The attorney may find it practical to use an interview sheet similar to the following sample:

FIGURE 7-1

```
                        INTERVIEW SHEET
Name_____Tel._____  Date of birth_____
Address_____
Name of spouse_____  Date of birth_____
Address_____
Date of Marriage_____    Place_____
```

Children: Age   Home:

1. _____ _____   Rented   per

2. _____ _____   Mortgage   per

3. _____ _____   Separated

4. _____ _____

Employment:

Wife   Employed_____   Salary_____ per_____

       Address_____   Tel._____

       Other income_____   Av. inc. for 6 mo.____per____

Hus.   Employed_____   Salary_____ per_____

       Address_____   Tel._____

       Other income_____   Av. inc. for 6 mo.____per____

Debts:

Name	Address	for	Total	Monthly
1. _____	_____	____	____	____
2. _____	_____	____	____	____
3. _____	_____	____	____	____
4. _____	_____	____	____	____

Previously married or divorced_____

Other children_____

Assets & Property:

1. _____

2. _____

3. _____

4. _____

Third party defendants

Filed or separated before

Prepare:

1. Complaint
                        Support   Per alimony   Custody
2. T. S. & A. $_____per____ $_____per_____

```
3.  Restraining order
4.  Motion to Vacate
5.  Answer
6.  Cross-Complaint
7.  Return to Maiden name
8.  Expense $_____
9.  Fee quoted $_____
```

You may conduct the initial interview with the client if the attorney wishes. This is a preliminary meeting in which you ask the client questions listed on the interview sheet. Make no attempt to advise the client about his or her case, its outcome, etc.; merely ask the prearranged questions. When all of the questions are answered, the client sees the attorney. The section at the end marked "Prepare" is for the attorney's use in instructing you.

FIGURE 7-2

IN THE COURT OF COMMON PLEAS, FRANKLIN COUNTY, OHIO DIVISION OF DOMESTIC RELATIONS

(Name and address of   :
   Plaintiff)
                                         :
                       Plaintiff

                                         :   Case No.
vs.

                                         :

(Name and address of
   Defendant)   :
                    Defendant   :

COMPLAINT

(1)   Plaintiff states that she has proper legal residence to maintain this action.

(2)   Plaintiff further states that she and Defendant were married at Columbus, Ohio, on September 30, 1946.

(3)   There is one child born issue of this marriage and his name is Brian, age 10 years.

(4)   Plaintiff and the Defendant are joint owners of real estate bounded and described as follows:

(described real estate)

(5)   Plaintiff states that the Defendant has been guilty of GROSS NEGLECT OF DUTY.

WHEREFORE,   Plaintiff demands that she be awarded a divorce from the defendant; be awarded custody of the minor child and child support; and such other relief as shall be proper and necessary including a reasonable sum for costs and attorney fees in this action.

Horace P. Black
BLACK & JONES
30 Main Street
Anytown, U.S.A.
Phone: 225-2241

Preparing the Pleadings

When the required information is taken on the interview sheet, the attorney may check off which pleadings are to be prepared by you. You may then take the interview sheet and prepare the necessary pleadings, gleaning the information from the sheet as you require it, using predictated forms from your form book and adapting them to the new case. Thus valuable dictation time is saved.

FIGURE 7-3

IN THE COURT OF COMMON PLEAS, FRANKLIN COUNTY, OHIO DIVISION OF DOMESTIC RELATIONS

(Name only of plaintiff)	:	
Plaintiff	:	
vs.	:	Case No.
(Name only of defendant)	:	
Defendant	:	

Supplemental Complaint

(1)   Plaintiff states that she is now and has been for more than one (1) year next immediately preceding the filing of the Supplemental Complaint a resident of the State of Ohio; that she has been for more than ninety (90) days, next immediately preceding the filing of this Supplemental Complaint, a bona fide resident of the County of Franklin, in the State of Ohio.

(2)   Plaintiff further states that she was married to the Defendant on the 1st day of May 1960, at_____, that two children _____, age _____, and _____, age _____ were born of this marriage.

(3)   Plaintiff states that on or about November 1, 19——, the parties reconciled conditioned upon the promise that the Defendant cease and desist in his aggressions against the Plaintiff; that, said Defendant has continued his acts of GROSS NEGLECT OF DUTY, the facts concerning the same will be more fully shown at the hearing of this cause.

WHEREFORE, Plaintiff prays that because of the aforesaid aggressions of the Defendant, she may be granted the custody and control of the minor children herein and that she may be granted a reasonable amount for the support of the children herein and for such further and general relief, as may be granted under the circumstances.

Horace P. Black
BLACK & JONES
30 Main Street
Anytown, U.S.A.

FIGURE 7-4

IN THE COURT OF COMMON PLEAS, FRANKLIN COUNTY, OHIO
DIVISION OF DOMESTIC RELATIONS

(Name of Plaintiff)   :

                    Plaintiff   :
    vs.   Case No.
(Name of defendant)   :

                    Defendant   :

ANSWER AND CROSS-COMPLAINT
        Now comes the defendant, _____, and in
answer to the Complaint of the Plaintiff, _____,
admits the residence of the Plaintiff; that the parties were
married in _____, and that no children were born as
issue of said marriage.

        Further answering, the Defendant denies each and every
allegation in the Plaintiff's Complaint not contained herein
or not in her Cross-Complaint specifically admitted to be
true.
                    CROSS-COMPLAINT
        Now comes the Defendant, _____, and
says that she is now and has been for more than one year last
past, a resident of the State of Ohio and that she is now,
and has been for at least 90 days immediately preceding the
filing of her cross-complaint herein, a bona fide resident
of the County of Franklin in said state.

        Defendant further states that she was married to the
Plaintiff, _____, on the _____day of _____,
_____, at _____, and that there were no children
born as issue of this marriage.

        For her cause of action, the Defendant says that while
she has at all times conducted herself as a good and dutiful
wife, Plaintiff has been guilty of GROSS NEGLECT OF DUTY
towards this Defendant, the details of which will be more fully
brought out at the trial of this cause.

        WHEREFORE, Defendant demands that because of the
aforesaid aggressions of the Plaintiff, the bonds of matrimony
existing between the Plaintiff and the Defendant, by virtue
of the marriage contract, be dissolved and that each of the
parties may be divorced from the other, that she may be
granted permanent alimony, that she may be granted expense
money, and for such further and general relief as may be
granted under the circumstances.

                              _____
                              Horace P. Black
                              BLACK & JONES
                              30 Main Street
                              Anytown, U. S. A.
                              Telephone: 225-2241

FIGURE 7-5

IN THE COURT OF COMMON PLEAS, FRANKLIN COUNTY, OHIO
DIVISION OF DOMESTIC RELATIONS

(Name of Plaintiff)   :

                    Plaintiff   :

vs.   :   Case No.

(Name of Defendant)   :

                    Defendant   :

M O T I O N

Now comes the Plaintiff, _____, and moves the
Court for an order restraining the Defendant, _____,
during the pendency of this action, from in any manner, or
by any means, disturbing, molesting or threatening the
Plaintiff or forcefully or violently placing his hands
upon her at any time or place.

This Motion is supported by the affidavit attached
hereto.

Respectfully submitted,

BLACK & JONES

By_____
        Horace P. Black

AFFIDAVIT
STATE OF OHIO, COUNTY OF FRANKLIN, SS:

_____, being first duly sworn, deposes
and states that on various occasions, Defendant, _____,
has been abusive to the Plaintiff in his conduct and remarks,
threatening her and Plaintiff believes, unless restrained,
Defendant will continue this course of action.

_____

        Sworn to before me and subscribed in my presence
this _____ day of _____, 19____.

_____

FIGURE 7-6

IN THE COURT OF COMMON PLEAS, FRANKLIN COUNTY, OHIO
DIVISION OF DOMESTIC RELATIONS

(Name of plaintiff)   :

                    Plaintiff   :

    vs.   :   CASE No.

(Name of Defendant)   :

                    Defendant   :

RESTRAINING ORDER

       This day this cause came on to be heard upon the
Motion of the Plaintiff requesting the Court for a
restraining order and upon due consideration thereof the
Court finds said Motion well taken and sustains the same.

       It is, THEREFORE, ORDERED, ADJUDGED AND DECREED
that the Defendant, _____, be and he is hereby
restrained from in any manner, or by any means, disturbing,
molesting or threatening the Plaintiff or forcefully or
violently placing his hands upon her at any time or place
until the further order of this Court.

       It is further ordered that a copy of this Order be
served upon the Defendant.

       For good cause shown, notice and bond are dispensed
with.

                         _____
                             JUDGE

Approved:
BLACK & JONES

By_____
Horace P. Black

FIGURE 7-7

IN THE COURT OF COMMON PLEAS, FRANKLIN COUNTY, OHIO
DIVISION OF DOMESTIC RELATIONS

(Name of Plaintiff)   :

              Plaintiff   :

  vs.   :   Case No.

(Name of Defendant)   :

             Defendant   :

M O T I O N

      Now comes the Plaintiff and moves the Court for an
order to require the Defendant to vacate the premises at
_____, Columbus, Ohio.

                                  _____
                                  Horace P. Black
                                  BLACK & JONES

Notice

To: (Name and address of defendant)

      You will take notice that the foregoing Motion will
come on for oral hearing before one of the Referees of the
Court of Domestic Relations, 50 East Mound Street, Columbus,
Ohio, on the _____day of _____, 19__, at _____
M.

                                  _____
                                  Attorney for Plaintiff

FIGURE 7-8

IN THE COURT OF COMMON PLEAS, FRANKLIN COUNTY, OHIO
DIVISION OF DOMESTIC RELATIONS

(Name of Plaintiff)   :

                        Plaintiff   :
                                                    Case No.
        vs.   :

(Name of Defendant)   :

                        Defendant   :

                        E N T R Y

        This day this cause came on to be heard upon the
Motion of the Plaintiff for an order to require the
Defendant to vacate the premises where the parties presently
live; and the Court, after hearing the testimony of the
parties and argument of counsel, finds said Motion well
taken and sustains the same.

        It is, THEREFORE, ORDERED, ADJUDGED AND DECREED
that the Defendant shall vacate the premises where the
parties presently live on or before _____ M. on the ____
day of _____, 19____.

                                    _____
                                          JUDGE

Approved:

_____
Attorney for Plaintiff

_____
Attorney for Defendant

FIGURE 7-9

IN THE COURT OF COMMON PLEAS, FRANKLIN COUNTY, OHIO
DIVISION OF DOMESTIC RELATIONS

(Name of Plaintiff)   :

               Plaintiff   :

vs.   :   Case No.

(Name of Defendant)   :

               Defendant   :

MOTION FOR RULE FOR CONTEMPT

      Now comes _____, the above-named Plaintiff
by her counsel, _____, and represents to the
Court that the above-named Defendant, _____, is in
default of the order heretofore made by this Court on the
_____day of _____, 19_____, by restraining the
Defendant from in any manner, or by any means, disturbing,
molesting or threatening the Plaintiff.

      WHEREFORE, said Plaintiff prays for a rule of the
Court ordering said Defendant, _____, to be cited to
appear before this Court and show cause why he should not
be punished for contempt for his default as above set forth.

                    Respectfully submitted,

                    BLACK & JONES

                    By_____
                    Horace P. Black

STATE OF OHIO, COUNTY OF FRANKLIN, SS:

      _____, being first duly sworn, deposes
and says that the facts stated and allegations contained in
the foregoing application are true as she verily believes.

_____

      Sworn to and subscribed before me this _____day
of _____, 19_____.

_____
                Notary Public

FIGURE 7-10

```
        IN THE COURT OF COMMON PLEAS, FRANKLIN COUNTY, OHIO
                 DIVISION OF DOMESTIC RELATIONS

(Name of Plaintiff)                    :

                 Plaintiff             :
                                             Case No.
    vs.                                :

(Name of Defendant)                    :

                 Defendant             :
```

E N T R Y

```
            This day this cause came on to be heard upon the
Motion of the Plaintiff for an order citing the Defendant
in contempt of this Court for his failure and refusal to
abide by the Court's previous ruling relative to child
support and expense money.

            The Court, being first duly advised in the premises,
finds said Motion to be well taken and hereby sustains the
same.

            It is, THEREFORE, ORDERED, ADJUDGED AND DECREED
by this Court that the Defendant, _____, be and he
is hereby ordered to appear before a Referee  of the Division
of Domestic Relations, 50 East Mound Street, Columbus, Ohio,
on the ____day of _____, 19__, at _____o'clock ___M.
to show cause, if any he has, why he should not be confined
in the Franklin County jail for contempt of this Court.


                              _____
                                        JUDGE

Approved:

BLACK & JONES

By_____
Horace P. Black
```

FIGURE 7-11

IN THE COURT OF COMMON PLEAS, FRANKLIN COUNTY,
OHIO DIVISION OF DOMESTIC RELATIONS

(Name of Plaintiff)   :

                           Plaintiff   :

    vs.

(Name of Defendant)   :   Case No.

         Defendant   :

MOTION

Now comes the Plaintiff and moves the Court for an Order reducing the amount of child support herein.

BLACK & JONES

By_____
Horace P. Black

Memorandum

The evidence to be presented at the hearing on this cause will show that the Plaintiff's income has been reduced substantially due to the fact that he is presently unemployed, making the existing order of child support inequitable.

Respectfully submitted,

_____
Horace P. Black
Attorney for Plaintiff

Notice

To: (Name of defendant)
    Address

You will take notice that the foregoing Motion will come for oral hearing before a Referee of the Court of Domestic Relations, Franklin County, Ohio, on the_____ day of _____
19_____.

_____
Horace P. Black

This will certify that a copy of the foregoing Motion, Memorandum, and Notice was mailed to_____, Attorney for Defendant, 8 East Broad Street, Columbus, Ohio, on the_____day of_____, 19_____.

_____
Horace P. Black

FIGURE 7-12

(To be sent to the City Editors of the daily newspapers.

Dear Sir:

It is our mutual desire that you not print notice of our
filing for divorce. The Complaint was filed on
_____, 19____. The style of the case is
"Shirley Jean Hobson vs. Lawrence J. Hobson."

Mr. Black, the attorney representing Shirley Jean Hobson,
has advised us that by mutually agreeing to the omission
of this notice, it will not appear in your newspaper.
Your favorable consideration of our request will be greatly
appreciated.

                                       Very truly yours,

                                       _____

                                       Shirley Jean Hobson

                                       _____

                                       Lawrence J. Hobson

Filing the Pleadings

The attorney may wish you to file his divorce actions. If so, become
familiar with the location of the Clerk's Office, prepare a check, or request it from the bookkeeper for the filing costs, and become familiar
with the procedure in your Domestic Relations Court for filing divorce actions.

Maintaining the Lawyer's Calendar

Use the diary system for recording hearing dates on divorces, and
employ a tickler to remind you and your boss a few days ahead of
time to prepare a final decree.

Arranging for Depositions

In cases of contested divorces, you may find it your responsibility to call a court stenographer in for a deposition. See that the time is convenient to opposing counsel and his client and any other persons involved.

Notifying the Client as to the Hearing Date

When the hearing date has been set, copy from a form letter in your form book to notify the client of the time and place and instruct her to come first to the attorney's office with the required number of witnesses. Include some prepared instructions to witnesses to aid the witnesses in performing their duty and to save the lawyer's time in instructing them. The lawyer may wish to also include in his letter some instructions on appropriate dress for the hearing as the judge may object to pant suits and hair curlers.

FIGURE 7-13

(Date)

Mrs. Elizabeth Jemson
606 Broad Street
Anytown, U. S. A.

Dear Mrs. Jemson:

You will find enclosed copies of the Pleadings we
filed on your behalf. Please note the hearing is
scheduled for April 22nd at 9:00 a.m. before the Court
Referee.

If we are unable to settle this matter prior to that
time, you should plan to meet with me in my office by
8:45 a.m. In the meantime, if you have any questions
or any additional information, please call.

Very truly yours,

BLACK & JONES

Horace P. Black

HPB:bt

FIGURE 7-14

Pointers to Witnesses

1. TELL THE TRUTH—A lie may lose the case. In a law suit, as in all other matters, honesty is the best policy. Telling the truth, however, means more than refraining from telling a deliberate falsehood. Telling the truth requires that a witness testify accurately about what he knows. If you tell the truth and tell it accurately, nobody can cross you up. Have no concern as to the effect of your testimony, just tell what you know and let the chips fall as they may.

2. DON'T GUESS—If you don't know, say you don't know. Do not testify as to what someone told you unless you are asked to relate a conversation.

3. Be sure that you understand the question before you attempt to give an answer. You can't possibly give a truthful and accurate answer unless you understand the question. If you don't understand the question, ask the lawyer to repeat it. He will probably ask the court reporter to read it back. If the question is not clear to you, say so.

4. TAKE YOUR TIME—Give the question such thought as it requires to understand it and formulate your answer and then give the answer.

5. ANSWER THE QUESTION that is asked and then stop. Don't volunteer information.

6. Talk loud enough so everybody can hear you. It is what the Court or jury hears that counts. Give your answer to the Court or jury trying the case and not to the lawyer questioning you. Don't chew gum and keep your hands away from your mouth. You can't speak distinctly while chewing gum or with your hand over your mouth.

7. Give an audible answer so the Court reporter can get it. Don't nod your head yes or no.

8. Don't look at the lawyer for help when you're on the stand. You're on your own. You won't get any help from the Judge either. If you look at the lawyer for your side when a question is asked on

cross-examination or for his approval after answering a question, the jury is bound to notice it and it will create a bad impression.

9. Beware of questions involving distances and time. If you make an estimate make sure that everyone understands you are estimating.

10. Know your name, where you live, how old you are and when you were married, etc.

11. Don't fence or argue with the lawyer on the other side. He has a right to question you, and if you give him some smart talk or give evasive answers the Judge may jump down your throat.

12. Don't lose your temper no matter how hard you are pressed. Lose your temper and you may lose the case. If you lose your temper you have played right into the hands of the other side.

13. Be courteous. Being courteous is one of the best ways to make a good impression on the court and jury. Be sure to answer "yes, sir" and "no, sir" and to address the Judge as "Your Honor."

14. If asked whether you have talked to the lawyer on your side, or to an investigator, admit it freely.

15. Avoid joking and wise cracks. A law suit is a serious matter.

16. Don't be afraid to look the jury in the eye and tell the story. Jurors are naturally sympathetic to the witness and want to hear what he has to say.

17. If you are a plaintiff in an accident case, be careful not to overemphasize the caution exercised for your own safety. Ordinary care is all that the law requires.

18. Give a positive answer when you can. Don't let the lawyer on the other side catch you by asking you whether you are willing to swear to your version of what you know by reason of seeing or hearing. If you were there and know what happened or didn't happen, don't be afraid to "swear" to it. You were "sworn" to tell the truth when you took the stand.

19. Do not try to "make a case." That is the lawyer's job. Just state the facts without embellishment.

20. Do not smoke while Court is in session.

NOTE: The foregoing Pointers to Witnesses are primarily for jury trial but can be adapted to Domestic Relations cases.

If your lawyer specializes in Family Law you may have to lend a sympathetic ear to the clients' problems. Most of what you hear will not be pleasant, some clients will be tearful and emotionally disturbed, but always maintain an impersonal, pleasant interest in the clients' tales of woe as often the client merely wants a shoulder to cry on.

Although each individual case is different, divorce matters become routine and you can handle them expertly after a little practice.

California "No-Fault" Forms

Since California (and more recently Florida) has pioneered in the "no-fault" divorce, a section is being included here with California forms in the event that other states follow suit.

California's present Code of Civil Procedure lists only two grounds for dissolution of a marriage or legal separation. They are as follows:

1. Irreconciliable differences that have caused irremedial breakdown of the marriage.
2. Incurable insanity. (Section 4506)

Irreconciliable differences are defined in Section 4507 as "those grounds which are determined by the court to be substantial reason for not continuing the marriage and which make it appear that the marriage should be dissolved."

The forms are preprinted on 8½x11 paper in contrast to the usual pleadings typed on legal cap. Following is a complete sample set of forms used in dissolving a marriage in California.

FIGURE 7-15

STATUTORY REQUIREMENTS AND INSTRUCTIONS FOR COMPLETING AND FILING FORM VS-243A, B AND C

Statutory requirements are that the triplicate three-part record (Form VS-243A, B and C) be completed with information obtained from the plaintiff and be furnished to the county clerk at the time of filing of * a petition for dissolution of marriage, legal separation, or for a judgment of nullity (Section 426a, Code of Civil Procedure and Chapter 6.5 of Division 9, Health and Safety Code.)

Confidentiality—Provision is made in the statutes that these records shall not be open to public inspection in the Office of the State Registrar of Vital Statistics or the offices of the county clerks (Section 10361, Health and Safety Code).

Items 1, 2, and 5 through 33 are to be completed on Forms VS-243A, B and C prior to filing the initial petition with the county clerk. The county clerk will complete items 3 and 4 at the time of filing the initial petition. These records will be considered completed when all blank spaces are filled in either with the requested information or the notation unknown (unk.) or not available (n.a.).

The Attorney's Record of Action for Dissolution of Marriage, Judgment of Nullity or Legal Separation (Form VS-242) is furnished as a working record for the use of the attorney and his staff in completing Forms VS-243A, B and C and may serve as the attorney's record of information in the action.

* Or within ten days thereafter and before the date of the first hearing

ATTORNEY'S RECORD OF ACTION FOR
DISSOLUTION OF MARRIAGE OR JUDGMENT
OF NULLITY OR LEGAL SEPARATION

STATE OF CALIFORNIA
DEPARTMENT OF PUBLIC HEALTH

BUREAU OF VITAL STATISTICS REGISTRATION
(REV 1-1-70) FORM VS-242

FIGURE 7-16

Name, Address and Telephone Number of Attorney(s)	Space Below for Use of Court Clerk Only

Attorney(s) for ....

SUPERIOR COURT OF CALIFORNIA, COUNTY OF SANTA CLARA

In re the marriage of

Petitioner:

        and

Respondent:

CASE NUMBER

PETITION (MARRIAGE)

1. This petition is for:

   ☐ Legal separation of the parties pursuant to:
      ☐ Civil Code Section 4506(1)
      ☐ Civil Code Section 4506(2)

   ☐ Dissolution of the marriage pursuant to:
      ☐ Civil Code Section 4506(1)
      ☐ Civil Code Section 4506(2)
   ....has been a resident of this state for at least six months and of this county for at least
       (Petitioner / Respondent)
   three months immediately preceding the filing of this petition.

   ☐ Nullity of the marriage pursuant to:
      ☐ Civil Code Section 4400
      ☐ Civil Code Section 4401
      ☐ Civil Code Section 4425(   )

2. Relevant statistical information for the purpose of this proceeding is:

   a. The parties were married on .... in ....
                  (Date)   *(Name of state or foreign country)*

   b. The date of separation is .... The number of years from date of marriage to date of
      separation is: .... years, ... months, ... days.

   c. There are .... children of this marriage including the following minor children:
       (Number)

Name	Birthdate	Age	Sex

   d. Husband's social security number is..................... Wife's social security number is.....................

Form Adopted by Rule 1281 of
Judicial Council of California
Effective January 1, 1970

PETITION (MARRIAGE)

3. The property subject to disposition by the court in this proceeding is:

   a. ☐ None

   b. ☐ Divided by agreement, which .... attached hereto
                     (is / is not)

   c. ☐ Stated below (or attached):
       1.
       2.
       3.
       4.
       5.
       6.
       7.
       8.

4. Petitioner requests that:

   a. ☐ Custody of children be awarded to
                                     (Petitioner / Respondent / other [specify])

   b. ☐ Support of children be awarded if need is found

   c. ☐ Spousal support .. be awarded ... . if need is found
              (not)   (Petitioner / Respondent)

   d. ☐ Property rights be determined as provided by law

   e. ☐ Attorneys' fees and costs ... ... be awarded..... ....-................if need is found
                        (not)   (Petitioner / Respondent)

and that the court inquire into the **status of** the marriage and render such judgments and make such injunctive or other orders as are appropriate.

5. A copy of the proposed judgment . .... . filed herewith.
                       (is / is not)

* I declare under penalty of perjury that the foregoing, including any attachments, is true and correct.

Executed on_____, at_____, California.
            (Date)   (Place)

_____   _____, Petitioner
      Attorney(s) for Petitioner

* A declaration under penalty of perjury must be executed within California. If document is executed outside California, attach an affidavit.

1545

FIGURE 7-17

Name, Address and Telephone No. of Attorney(s)   Space Below for Use of Court Clerk Only

Attorney(s) for...

SUPERIOR COURT OF CALIFORNIA, COUNTY OF SANTA CLARA

....(Insert post office and street address of court or branch court).......................

In re the marriage of   CASE NUMBER

Petitioner:
                        and

Respondent: SUMMONS (MARRIAGE)

ı o the Respondent:

The petitioner has filed a petition concerning your marriage. You may file a written response within thirty days of the date that this summons is served on you. If you fail to file a written response within such time, your default may be entered and the court may enter a judgment containing injunctive or other orders concerning division of property, spousal support, child custody, child support, attorneys' fees, costs, and such other relief as may be granted by the court.

If you wish to seek the advice of an attorney in this matter, you should do so promptly so that your written response, if any, may be filed on time.

Dated _____   _____ GEORGE E. FOWLES _____ , Clerk

                                        By _____ , Deputy

    (SEAL)

The response and other permitted papers must be in writing and in the form prescribed by the California Rules of Court. They must be filed in this court with the proper filing fee and proof of service of a copy of each on petitioner.

The time when a summons is deemed served on a party may vary depending on the method of service. For example, see Code of Civil Procedure §§ 413.10 through 415.40.
                        (See reverse side for Proof of Service)

Form Adopted by Rule 1283 of
 Judicial Council of California
Revised Effective July 1, 1970   **SUMMONS (MARRIAGE)**

PROOF OF SERVICE (See Instruction Sheet)

I served the summons and ☐ Petition (Marriage), ☐ Proposed Judgment (Marriage), ☐ *Blank* Confidential Questionnaire (Marriage),
☐ Order to Show Cause and Declarations re Order to Show Cause (Marriage),
☐ 3 *Blank* Order to Show Cause and Declarations re Order to Show Cause (Marriage), as follows:

1. Name:

2. Person served and title:

3. Person with whom left; title or
   relationship to person served:

4. Date and time of delivery:

5. Mailing date; type of mail:

6. Address, city and state (when
   required, indicate whether address
   is home or business):

7. Manner of service: (Check applicable box for each person served and complete this form.)

☐ **(Personal service)** By handing copies to the person served. (C.C.P. § 415.10.)

☐ **(Substituted service on corporation, unincorporated association (including partnership), or public entity)** By leaving, during usual office hours, copies in the office of the person served with the person who apparently was in charge and thereafter mailing (by first-class mail, postage prepaid) copies to the person served at the place where the copies were left. (C.C.P. § 415.20(a).) Place of mailing: . . . . : . .

☐ **(Substituted service on natural person, minor, incompetent, or candidate)** By leaving copies at the dwelling house, usual place of abode, or usual place of business of the person served in the presence of a competent member of the household or a person apparently in charge of his office or place of business, at least 18 years of age, who was informed of the general nature of the papers, and thereafter mailing (by first-class mail, postage prepaid) copies to the person served at the place where the copies were left. (C.C.P. § 415.20(b). Attach separate declaration or affidavit stating acts relied on to establish reasonable diligence in first attempting personal service.) Place of mailing: . . . .

☐ **(Mail and acknowledgment service)** By mailing (by first-class mail or airmail) copies to the person served, together with two copies of the form of notice and acknowledgment and a return envelope, postage prepaid, addressed to the sender. (C.C.P. § 415.30. Attach written acknowledgment of receipt.) Place of mailing: . . . .

☐ **(Certified or registered mail service)** By mailing to address outside California (by registered or certified airmail with return receipt requested) copies to the person served. (C.C.P. § 415.40. Attach signed return receipt or other evidence of actual delivery to the person served.) Place of mailing: . . . .

☐ **(Other--C.C.P. §§ 413.10, 413.30, 417.10--417.30--Attach separate pages if necessary):**

At the time of service I was at least 18 years of age and not a party to this action.

Fee for service $ . . . . , ... , Mileage $ . . . . , Notary $ . . . . , Total $ . . . .

(To be completed in California by process server,
other than a sheriff, marshal or constable*)

(To be completed in California by
sheriff, marshal or constable*)

I declare under penalty of perjury that the foregoing is true and correct and this declaration was executed on (Insert date): _____

at (Insert place) : _____ , California.
(Type or print name, address and telephone no.)

I certify that the foregoing is true and correct and this certificate was executed on (Insert date): _____

(Type or print name, title, county and , when applicable,
Municipal or Justice Court District)

Signature: _____

Signature: _____

*This declaration or certificate of service must be executed within California. (C.C.P § 2015.5). A proof of service executed outside California must be made by affidavit.

FIGURE 7-18

Name, Address and Telephone Number of Attorney(s)	Space Below for Use of Court Clerk Only
Attorney(s) for	

SUPERIOR COURT OF CALIFORNIA, COUNTY OF SANTA CLARA

In re the marriage of	CASE NUMBER
Petitioner: and Respondent:	☒ PETITIONER'S ☐ RESPONDENT'S CONFIDENTIAL QUESTIONNAIRE (MARRIAGE)

The information supplied by you in this questionnaire is strictly confidential and may be used only by the court. Answer all the questions and be as fair and impartial as possible. (You may answer questions 1 through 29 by attaching a copy of Bureau of Vital Statistics Form VS-243A as filed with the court.)

☐ A copy of Form VS-243A is attached.

1. Type of proceeding...

HUSBAND'S PERSONAL INFORMATION

2. Name of husband...   3. Date of birth ....
　　　　　　　　　(First)　　(Middle)　　　　(Last)

4. Present address...
　　　　　　　　(Number and Street)　　　　　　　(City or Town)　　　(County)　　　(State)

5. Length of stay in California....................years.

6. Birthplace...   7. Present or last occupation ....
　　　　　　　(State or Country)

8. Highest school grade completed . . ..   9. Race........ ....   10. Religion................................

11. Number of previous marriages.........................   12. How dissolved. ....
　　　　　　　　　　　　　　　　　　　　　　　　　　　　　　　(Death / Legal proceeding)

WIFE'S PERSONAL INFORMATION

13. Name of wife ....   14. Date of birth ....
　　　　　　　(First)　　(Middle)　　　(Last)

15. Present address. ... .
　　　　　　　　(Number and Street)　　　　　　(City or Town)　　　(County)　　　(State)

16. Length of stay in California......................years.

17. Birthplace ....   18. Present or last occupation ....
　　　　　　(State or Country)

19. Highest school grade completed......................................   20. Race..... ....   21. Religion .. ..

22. Number of previous marriages..... .. . .   23. How dissolved ....
　　　　　　　　　　　　　　　　　　　　　　　　　　　　　　　(Death / Legal proceeding)

Form Adopted by Rule 1284 of
Judicial Council of California
Effective January 1, 1970   **CONFIDENTIAL QUESTIONNAIRE (MARRIAGE)**

MARRIAGE AND FAMILY INFORMATION

24. Place of marriage .... 25. Date of marriage ....
               (City)   (County)   (State or Country)

26. Number of children of this marriage .... 27. Ages of these children ....

28. Are you living together now? .... 29. If not, when did you separate? ....

30. Husband's age at time of this marriage .... 31. If previously married give the age at the time of each ....

32. Wife's age at time of this marriage . ... 33. If previously married give the age at the time of each ....

34. The children of this marriage are now living with ....

35. Are there children not of this marriage? ....
                                (yes / no)

    a. Husband's children: ...., now living with ....
                       (Number)   (Ages)

    b. Wife's children: .... , now living with ....
                  (Number)   (Ages)

36. Are the children now living with the husband or wife aware of your difficulties? ....

37. Is the wife pregnant now? ....

38 When you were growing up did your (or your spouse's) parents or step-parents have any serious marital difficulties?
    ----

39. Did they ever separate or get a divorce? ....

40. If so, how old were you (or your spouse) at the time? ....

41. Who was the first person other than your spouse with whom you discussed your marital problems (parents, relative,

    minister, attorney, doctor, neighbor, etc.)? ....

42. Have you or your spouse ever sought professional counseling for this marriage? . ...**If so, specify from whom**
                                                              (yes/no)
    (psychiatrist, psychologist, clergyman, licensed marriage counselor, social worker) ... .

43. For how long? ....

44. What do you feel is wrong with this marriage? ....

    ....

    ....

    ....

45. Would you like counseling? ....
                            (yes / no)

Date _____   _____ (Petitioner/Respondent)
                                                   (Signature)

FIGURE 7-19

Name, Address and Telephone Number of Attorney(s)   Space Below for Use of Court Clerk Only

Attorney(s) for ....

SUPERIOR COURT OF CALIFORNIA, COUNTY OF SANTA CLARA

In re the marriage of   CASE NUMBER

Petitioner:
                                  and
Respondent: ☐ **PETITIONER'S**   ☒ **RESPONDENT'S**
                                                 CONFIDENTIAL QUESTIONNAIRE (MARRIAGE)

The information supplied by you in this questionnaire is strictly confidential and may be used only by the court. Answer all the questions and be as fair and impartial as possible. (You may answer questions 1 through 29 by attaching a copy of Bureau of Vital Statistics Form VS-243A as filed with the court.)

☐ A copy of Form VS-243A is attached.

1. Type of proceeding ....

HUSBAND'S PERSONAL INFORMATION

2. Name of husband.. ....   3. Date of birth ....
                    (First)   (Middle)   (Last)

4. Present address. ....
                    (Number and Street)   (City or Town)   (County)   (State)

5. Length of stay in California................years.

6. Birthplace ....   7. Present or last occupation ....
                    (State or Country)

8. Highest school grade completed ....   9. Race .... 10. Religion.................

11. Number of previous marriages ....   12. How dissolved ....
                                                                            (Death / Legal proceeding)

WIFE'S PERSONAL INFORMATION

13. Name of wife ....   14. Date of birth ....
                    (First)   (Middle)   (Last)

15. Present address ....
                    (Number and Street)   (City or Town)   (County)   (State)

16. Length of stay in California.................years.

17. Birthplace ....   18. Present or last occupation.............
                    (State or Country)

19. Highest school grade completed.................   20. Race .... 21. Religion ....

22. Number of previous marriages ....   23. How dissolved ....
                                                                            (Death / Legal proceeding)

Form Adopted by Rule 1284 of
Judicial Council of California   **CONFIDENTIAL QUESTIONNAIRE (MARRIAGE)**
Effective January 1, 1970

MARRIAGE AND FAMILY INFORMATION

24. Place of marriage... 25. Date of marriage ....
                           (City)   (County)   (State or Country)

26. Number of children of this marriage...................... 27. Ages of these children.. ....

28. Are you living together now?............................... 29. If not, when did you separate?.....................................

30. Husband's age at time of this marriage............... 31. If previously married give the age at the time of each...............

32. Wife's age at time of this marriage.... .... 33. If previously married give the age at the time of each...............

34. The children of this marriage are now living with ....

35. Are there children not of this marriage?.. ....
                                    (yes / no)

    a. Husband's children: ...., now living with ....
                   (Number)   (Ages)

    b. Wife's children: ...., now living with...
                (Number)   (Ages)

36. Are the children now living with the husband or wife aware of your difficulties?...................

37. Is the wife pregnant now?...................

38 When you were growing up did your (or your spouse's) parents or step-parents have any serious marital difficulties?
    _____

39. Did they ever separate or get a divorce?...................

40. If so, how old were you (or your spouse) at the time?...................

41. Who was the first person other than your spouse with whom you discussed your marital problems (parents, relative,

    minister, attorney, doctor, neighbor, etc.)?...

42. Have you or your spouse ever sought professional counseling for this marriage? .. ..If so, specify from whom
                                                                    (yes/no)
    (psychiatrist, psychologist, clergyman, licensed marriage counselor, social worker).......................................

43. For how long?...........................

44. What do you feel is wrong with this marriage?........... ....

  ... .

....

 . ...

45. Would you like counseling?...................
               (yes / no)

Date_____   _____(Petitioner/Respondent)
                                          (Signature)

FIGURE 7-20

Name, Address and Telephone Number of Attorney(s)

Space Below for Use of Court Clerk Only

Attorney(s) for ....

SUPERIOR COURT OF CALIFORNIA, COUNTY OF SANTA CLARA

In re the marriage of

Petitioner:

and

Respondent:

CASE NUMBER:

☐ **REQUEST**   ☐ **RESPONSE**
RE ORDER TO SHOW CAUSE, AND
☐ **PETITIONER'S**   ☐ **RESPONDENT'S**
DECLARATIONS RE ORDER TO
SHOW CAUSE (MARRIAGE)

TO: ☐ Petitioner   ☐ Respondent   ☐ .   .   ..
(Specify)

ORDER TO SHOW CAUSE

☐ You are ordered to appear in this court, located at ..., ...,
(Street address and City)

on ..   .. at   .   . .m., Department or Room No.   , to give any legal reason why
(Date)   (Time)

certain orders requested by . .. .   as set forth in the Declarations below should not be made by
(Petitioner / Respondent)

this court.

☐ An endorsed copy of this Order and Declarations re Order to Show Cause (Marriage), together with three blank copies
of this form, must be served on you at least   days before the date of the above hearing. You must complete
and serve and file copies of this form at   .. . . the hearing.
(the time of/least ..   days before)

☐ An endorsed copy of this Order and Declarations re Order to Show Cause (Marriage) must be served on you at least
. .. . days before the date of the hearing set forth above. If you wish to respond, you must serve and file your
response at .... the hearing.
(the time of/least   days before)

☐ **(Ex parte order)**   Pending a hearing in this matter, the court further orders as follows:

Dated ....
Judge of the Superior Court

Form Adopted by Rule 1285 of
Judicial Council of California
Effective January 1, 1970

(See reverse side for Declarations)
ORDER TO SHOW CAUSE and
DECLARATIONS RE ORDER TO SHOW CAUSE (MARRIAGE)

DECLARATIONS RE ORDER TO SHOW CAUSE

☐ 1. **Custody of children:** ☐ Order ☐ Modification

I request/consent that custody of our children be awarded to .... : (Insert name and age of each child)

	Amount sought (or now paid if modification sought)	Modified amount sought		Amount sought (or now paid if modification sought)	Modified amount sought
☐ 2. **Support of children:**			☐ 4. **Attorneys' fees:**		
[ ] Order ☐ Modification			☐ Order ☐ Modification		
I request/consent that $			I request/consent that $		
monthly per child be paid for support,			be paid for attorneys' fees, payable*		
payable* ... Number of			. (Complete Part B) $	$	
children . Total monthly sup-			☐ 5. **Court costs:**		
port (Complete Part A below) . . . $	$		☐ Order ☐ Modification		
			I request/consent that $		
☐ 3. **Support for spouse:**			be paid for court costs, payable*		
☐ Order ☐ Modification			. (Complete Part B) $	$	
I request/consent that $			☐ 6. **Injunctive/other order:**		
monthly be paid for spousal support,			☐ Order ☐ Modification		
payable* ... . (Complete			I seek an		
Part A below) . . . . $	$		(injunctive/specify other)		
			order as follows: (Complete Part B)		

* Specify proposed manner of payment (weekly, monthly, etc.).

Part A. Supporting Financial Statement

(a) Gross monthly income, payable	Husband	Wife		(c) Total monthly expenses:	Husband	Wife	Children
(specify): ... ... $	$			1. Rent or mortgage payments (residence) $	$	$	
				2. Food			
(b) Net monthly income . . . . $	$			3. Transportation			
Itemize deductions from gross:	Husband	Wife		4. Utilities			
Income taxes . . . . $	$			5. Laundry and cleaning			
Social Security				6. Clothes			
Unemployment insurance . . .				7. Medical and dental			
Medical or other insurance . .				8. Insurance			
Union or other dues				9. Child care			
Retirement or pension fund . .				10. Incidentals			
Savings plan				11. Payment of child/spousal support re			
Other (specify):				prior marriage			
...				12. Other (specify)			
... .				13. Installment payments on existing debts			
... ...				as itemized below **			
Total deductions . . . . $	$			Total $	$	$	
** Creditor's Name	For	Monthly Payment	Balance	** Creditor's Name	For	Monthly Payment	Balance
		$	$			$	$

(d) All property of the parties known to me includes the following:

Cash on hand . . . . . $	Money in credit union account(s) . . . $	Value of real estate . . . $
Money in checking account(s) .	Money in any other account(s) or deposit(s)	Value of all other property _____
Money in savings account(s) .	Value of any stocks and bonds	Total Property: . . . . $

NOTE: Bring with you income tax returns, payroll statements, payroll check stubs, or other documents necessary to verify your income.

Part B. Supporting Information re custody / attorneys' fees / court costs / injunctive or other order.

* I declare under penalty of perjury that the foregoing, including any attachments, is true and correct.

Executed on_____, at_____, California.

      (Date)   (Place)

___ _____(Petitioner/Respondent)

    Attorney(s) for Petitioner (Respondent)

* A declaration under penalty of perjury must be executed within California. If document is executed outside California, attach on affidavit.

FIGURE 7-21

Name, Address and Telephone Number of Attorney(s)	Space Below for Use of Court Clerk Only

Attorney(s) for..

SUPERIOR COURT OF CALIFORNIA, COUNTY OF SANTA CLARA

In re the marriage of	CASE NUMBER
Petitioner:	
and	
Respondent:	**RESPONSE (MARRIAGE)**

1. This response is for:

   ☐ Reconciliation of the parties

   ☐ Legal separation of the parties pursuant to:
       ☐ Civil Code Section 4506(1)
       ☐ Civil Code Section 4506(2)

   ☐ Dissolution of the marriage pursuant to:
       ☐ Civil Code Section 4506(1)
       ☐ Civil Code Section 4506(2)
   ....has been a resident of this state for at least six months and of this county for at least
       (Petitioner / Respondent)
   three months immediately preceding the filing of this petition.

   ☐ Nullity of the marriage pursuant to:
       ☐ Civil Code Section 4400
       ☐ Civil Code Section 4401
       ☐ Civil Code Section 4425(   )

2. The relevant statistical information in the petition is......................... . . (If incorrect, complete the following)
                     (correct / incorrect)

   a. The parties were married on ....in...
                    (Date)   (Name of state or foreign country)

   b. The date of separation is .... The number of years from date of marriage to date of
   separation is: ... years, ...months, ...days.

   c. There are .. children of this marriage including the following minor children:
      (Number)

Name	Birthdate	Age	Sex

   d. Husband's soc.' 'ecurity number is.. .... Wife's social security number is.......................................

Form Adopted by Ru . d2 of
Judicial Council of C 'c ia
Effective January 1, 1970
                                   RESPONSE (MARRIAGE)

3. The statement in the petition of property subject to disposition by the court in this proceeding is..
   (correct / incorrect)

   (If incorrect, complete the following) The property subject to disposition by the court in this proceeding is:

   a. ☐ None

   b. ☐ Divided by agreement, which................attached hereto
      (is / is not)

   c. ☐ Stated below (or attached):
      1.
      2.
      3.
      4.
      5.
      6.
      7.
      8.

4. Respondent requests that:

   a. ☐ Custody of children be awarded to ....
      (Petitioner / Respondent / other [specify])

   b. ☐ Support of children be awarded if need is found

   c. ☐ Spousal support............ be awarded............................ if need is found
      (not)   (Petitioner / Respondent)

   d. ☐ Property rights be determined as provided by law

   e. ☐ Attorneys' fees and costs...............be awarded.............................. if need is found
      (not)   (Petitioner / Respondent)

   and that the court inquire into the status of the marriage and render such judgments and make such injunctive or other orders as are appropriate.

5. Respondent...................................with Petitioner's proposed judgment, if any, filed with the petition. If not, a copy of
   (concurs / does not concur)

   Respondent's proposed judgment............ filed herewith.
   (is / is not)

   * I declare under penalty of perjury that the foregoing, including any attachments, is true and correct.

   Executed on_____, at_____, California.
   (Date)   (Place)

   _____   _____, Respondent
   Attorney(s) for Respondent

   * A declaration under penalty of perjury must be executed within California. If document is executed outside California, attach an affidavit.

FIGURE 7-22

Name, Address and Telephone Number of Attorney(s)   Space Below for Use of Court Clerk Only

Attorney(s) for ....

SUPERIOR COURT OF CALIFORNIA, COUNTY OF SANTA CLARA

In re the marriage of

Petitioner:

and

Respondent:

Default entered as requested, on.................................
By ....
☐ Default NOT entered as requested (state reason on reverse side).

CASE NUMBER:

**REQUEST AND DECLARATIONS
RE DEFAULT (MARRIAGE)**

I. REQUEST TO ENTER DEFAULT

TO THE CLERK: Please enter the default of the respondent who has been regularly served with process and who has failed to appear or respond to the petition within the time allowed by law.

Date_____   _____
                                                          Attorney(s) for Petitioner

II. DECLARATION OF NON-MILITARY STATUS

Respondent is not in the military service or in the military service of the United States as defined in Section 101 of the Soldiers' and Sailors' Relief Act of 1940, as amended, and not entitled to the benefits of such act.
 * I declare under penalty of perjury that the foregoing is true and correct.

Executed on_____,   _____
                (Date)   (Signature of Declarant)
at_____, California.   _____
            (Place)   (Type or print name of Declarant)

III. DECLARATION RE MEMORANDUM OF COSTS

Clerk's Filing Fees . . . . $..................
Process-Server's Fees . . . . $..................
Notary Fees . . . . $..................
      . . . . $..................
      . . . . $..................
      . . . . $..................

 I am the _____ party who claims these costs. To the best of my knowledge and belief the foregoing items of cost are correct and have been necessarily incurred in this proceeding.

 * I declare under penalty of perjury that the foregoing is true and correct.

Executed on_____,   _____
                (Date)   (Signature of Declarant)
at_____, California.   _____
            (Place)   (Type or print name of Declarant)

(See reverse side for Financial Statement and Declaration of Mailing)

Form Adopted by Rule 1286 of
Judicial Council of California   **REQUEST AND DECLARATIONS RE DEFAULT (MARRIAGE)**
Effective January 1, 1970

IV. FINANCIAL STATEMENT

The value of each asset and the amount of each obligation subject to disposition by the court is:

Description of asset /obligation	Asset	Obligation
	$	$

* I declare under penalty of perjury that the foregoing, including any attachments, is true and correct.

Executed on_____,   _____
                         (Date)   (Signature of Petitioner-Declarant)

at_____, California.   _____
                 (Place)   (Type or print name)

V. DECLARATION OF MAILING

On the date stated below, I mailed (by first-class mail or airmail, postage prepaid) a copy of this Request and Declarations re Default to the respondent's attorney of record, or if none, to respondent at his last known address, addressed as follows:

* I declare under penalty of perjury that the foregoing is true and correct.

Executed on_____,   _____
                         (Date)   (Signature of Petitioner or Attorney)

at_____, California.   _____
                 (Place)   (Type or print name)

* A declaration under penalty of perjury must be executed within California. If document is executed outside California, attach an affidavit.

Name, Address and Telephone Number of Attorney(s)   Space Below for Use of Court Clerk Only

Attorney(s) for ....

SUPERIOR COURT OF CALIFORNIA, COUNTY OF SANTA CLARA

In re the marriage of   CASE NUMBER

Petitioner:

                              and

Respondent: **INTERLOCUTORY JUDGMENT OF**
                                                                   DISSOLUTION OF MARRIAGE

This proceeding was heard on............. .... _. before the Honorable   .. .. ,
                                    (Date)

Department No.......................

The court acquired jurisdiction of the respondent on...... .. .. by:
                                                    (Date)

☐ Service of process on that date, respondent not having appeared within the time permitted by law.

☐ Service of process on that date and respondent having appeared.

☐ Respondent on that date having appeared.

The court orders that an interlocutory judgment be entered declaring that the parties are entitled to have their marriage dissolved. This interlocutory judgment does not constitute a final dissolution of marriage and the parties are still married and will be, and neither party may remarry, until a final judgment of dissolution is entered.

The court also orders that, unless both parties file their consent to a dismissal of this proceeding, a final judgment of dissolution be entered upon proper application of either party or on the court's own motion after the expiration of at least six months from the date the court acquired jurisdiction of the respondent. The final judgment shall include such other and further relief as may be necessary to a complete disposition of this proceeding, but entry of the final judgment shall not deprive this court of its jurisdiction over any matter expressly reserved to it in this or the final judgment until a final disposition is made of each such matter.

Dated_____ _____ _____ ___ _   ___ ...._ ____ _ ___ _____
                                                        Judge of the Superior Court

Form Adopted by Rule 1287 of   **INTERLOCUTORY JUDGMENT OF**
Judicial Council of California   **DISSOLUTION OF MARRIAGE**
Effective January 1, 1970

FIGURE 7-24

Name, Address and Telephone Number of Attorney(s)

Space Below for Use of Court Clerk Only

Attorney(s) for ....

SUPERIOR COURT OF CALIFORNIA, COUNTY OF SANTA CLARA

In re the marriage of

CASE NUMBER

Petitioner:

                and

Respondent:

NOTICE OF ENTRY OF JUDGMENT (MARRIAGE)

You are notified that the following judgment in this cause was entered in Judgment Book No...............................,

page.. .. .   ., on. ... ., ...:
                                (Date)

☐ Interlocutory Judgment of Dissolution of Marriage

☐ Final Judgment of Dissolution of Marriage

☐ Final Judgment of Legal Separation

☐ Final Judgment of Nullity

GEORGE E. FOWLES, **Clerk**

By_____, Deputy

DECLARATION OF MAILING

On the date stated below, I mailed (by first-class mail or airmail, postage prepaid) a copy of this Notice of Entry of Judgment (Marriage) to the parties, addressed as follows:

GEORGE E. FOWLES, **Clerk**

Dated __ _____   By_____, Deputy

Form Adopted by Rule 1290 of
Judicial Council of California   **NOTICE OF ENTRY OF JUDGMENT (MARRIAGE)**
Effective January 1, 1970

FIGURE 7-25

Name, Address and Telephone Number of Attorney(s)   Space Below for Use of Court Clerk Only

Attorney(s) for   .. ..

SUPERIOR COURT OF CALIFORNIA, COUNTY OF SANTA CLARA

In re the marriage of   CASE NUMBER

Petitioner:

        and

Respondent: **REQUEST AND DECLARATIONS FOR FINAL
                                                      JUDGMENT OF DISSOLUTION OF MARRIAGE**

The court acquired jurisdiction of the respondent on   ..   .... by:
                                                               (Date)

☐ Service of process on that date, respondent not having appeared within the time permitted by law.

☐ Service of process on that date and respondent having appeared.

☐ Respondent on that date having appeared.

An interlocutory judgment of dissolution of marriage was granted by this court on   . .   .. , and
                                                                                    (Date)

entered in Judgment Book No.   , page   , on   . .. .
                                                              (Date)

Since the granting of the interlocutory judgment, each of the following is true of my own knowledge except as stated below:

(a) The parties have not become reconciled and have not agreed to dismiss this proceeding.

(b) No motion to set aside or annul the interlocutory judgment or suit brought therefor is pending and undetermined, and no appeal has been taken or is pending therefrom, and said judgment has become final.

☐ I request that final judgment be entered.

☐ I request that final judgment be entered nunc pro tunc as of   for the following reason:
                                                                 (Date)

* I declare under penalty of perjury that the foregoing is true and correct.

Executed on _   ___ _____ ___, at   ___._____ _____ __ ._____, Caifornia.
                (Date)   (Place)

_____ __ ___ __ _____. ___ ___ ___   _____
    Attorney(s) for   (Signature of Petitioner/Respondent)
                      (Petitioner/Respondent)
* This declaration under penalty of perjury must be executed within California. If document is executed outside California, attach an affidavit.

Form Adopted by Rule 1288 of   **REQUEST AND DECLARATIONS FOR FINAL**
  Judicial Council of California   **JUDGMENT OF DISSOLUTION OF MARRIAGE**
    Effective January 1, 1970

FIGURE 7-26

Name, Address and Telephone Number of Attorney(s)

Space Below for Use of Court Clerk Only

Attorney(s) for ....

SUPERIOR COURT OF CALIFORNIA, COUNTY OF SANTA CLARA

In re the marriage of

Petitioner:

and

Respondent:

CASE NUMBER

FINAL JUDGMENT (MARRIAGE) OF

(LEGAL SEPARATION/NULLITY/DISSOLUTION)

This proceeding was heard on .... (Date) .... before the Honorable .... ,

Department No. ....

The court acquired jurisdiction of the respondent on .... (Date) .... by:

☐ Service of process on that date, respondent not having appeared within the time permitted by law.

☐ Service of process on that date and respondent having appeared.

☐ Respondent on that date having appeared.

The court orders that:

☐ Pursuant to ☐ Civil Code Section 4506(1) or ☐ Civil Code Section 4506(2), a Judgment of Legal Separation and such other orders as are set out below be entered.

☐ Pursuant to ☐ Civil Code Section 4400, ☐ Civil Code Section 4401, or ☐ Civil Code Section 4425( ), a Judgment of Nullity and such other orders as are set out below be entered, and that the parties be restored to the status of unmarried persons.

☐ Pursuant to ☐ Civil Code Section 4506(1) or ☐ Civil Code Section 4506(2), a Final Judgment of Dissolution be entered, and that all of the provisions of the interlocutory judgment, which was entered on .... , except as otherwise set out below, be made binding the same as if set forth in full, and that the parties be restored to the status of unmarried persons.

Dated_____

_____
Judge of the Superior Court

Form Adopted by Rule 1289 of
Judicial Council of California
Effective January 1, 1970

FINAL JUDGMENT (MARRIAGE)

FIGURE 7-27

See Attorney's Record of Action for Dissolution of Marriage, Judgment of Nullity or Legal Separation (VS-242) for instructions regarding this record.

CERTIFICATE OF REGISTRY OF FINAL DECREE OF DISSOLUTION OF MARRIAGE OR JUDGMENT OF NULLITY OR LEGAL SEPARATION	(TO BE COMPLETED BY COUNTY CLERK) 3 CASE NUMBER

STATE FILE NUMBER			

	1 TYPE OF PETITION (SPECIFY DISSOLUTION OF MARRIAGE. JUDGMENT OF NULLITY OR LEGAL SEPARATION)	2 COUNTY IN WHICH PETITION FILED	4 DATE PETITION FILED—MONTH. DAY. YEAR
HUSBAND PERSONAL DATA	5A NAME OF HUSBAND—FIRST NAME / 5B MIDDLE NAME / 5C LAST NAME		6 DATE OF BIRTH—MONTH DAY YEAR
	7A PRESENT ADDRESS—STREET AND NUMBER / 7B CITY OR TOWN / 7C COUNTY (IF OUTSIDE CALIFORNIA GIVE STATE)		7D LENGTH OF STAY IN CALIFORNIA _____ YEARS
	8 BIRTHPLACE (STATE OR FOREIGN COUNTRY) / 10A PRESENT OR LAST OCCUPATION / 10B KIND OF BUSINESS OR INDUSTRY		
	11 HIGHEST SCHOOL GRADE COMPLETED / 12 COLOR OR RACE / 13 RELIGIOUS DENOMINATION		14 NUMBER OF PREVIOUS MARRIAGES TERMINATED BY DEATH _____ LEGAL PROCEEDINGS _____
WIFE PERSONAL DATA	15A MAIDEN NAME OF WIFE—FIRST NAME / 15B MIDDLE NAME / 15C LAST NAME		16 DATE OF BIRTH—MONTH. DAY. YEAR
	17A PRESENT ADDRESS—STREET AND NUMBER / 17B CITY OR TOWN / 17C COUNTY (IF OUTSIDE CALIFORNIA. GIVE STATE)		17D LENGTH OF STAY IN CALIFORNIA _____ YEARS
	18 BIRTHPLACE (STATE OR FOREIGN COUNTRY) / 20A PRESENT OR LAST OCCUPATION / 20B KIND OF BUSINESS OR INDUSTRY		
	21 HIGHEST SCHOOL GRADE COMPLETED / 22 COLOR OR RACE / 23 RELIGIOUS DENOMINATION		24 NUMBER OF PREVIOUS MARRIAGES TERMINATED BY DEATH _____ LEGAL PROCEEDINGS _____
PLACE AND DATE OF MARRIAGE	25A PLACE OF MARRIAGE—CITY OR TOWN	25B COUNTY (IF OUTSIDE CALIFORNIA. GIVE STATE)	26 DATE OF MARRIAGE—MONTH DAY YEAR

27 NAMES. BIRTHPLACES. AND BIRTHDATES OF LIVING CHILDREN OF THIS MARRIAGE (BORN OR ADOPTED)

LIVING CHILDREN OF THIS MARRIAGE	FIRST NAME AND MIDDLE INITIAL	PLACE OF BIRTH (STATE OR FOREIGN COUNTRY)	DATE OF BIRTH MONTH. DAY. YEAR	FIRST NAME AND MIDDLE INITIAL	PLACE OF BIRTH (STATE OR FOREIGN COUNTRY)	DATE OF BIRTH MONTH. DAY. YEAR

SEPARATION	28A RESIDENCE AT TIME OF SEPARATION—CITY OR TOWN	28B COUNTY (IF OUTSIDE CALIFORNIA GIVE STATE)	29 DATE OF SEPARATION—MONTH DAY YEAR
LEGAL GROUNDS FOR PETITION	30 LEGAL GROUNDS ON WHICH PETITION FILED		31A PETITIONER (SPECIFY HUSBAND OR WIFE)
CERTIFICATION OF PETITIONER	I have reviewed the above stated information and hereby certify that it is true and correct to the best of my knowledge and belief.	31B SIGNATURE OF PETITIONER ▶	31C DATE OF SIGNATURE
ATTORNEY FOR PETITIONER	32 NAME OF ATTORNEY FOR PETITIONER	33 ADDRESS—STREET AND NUMBER CITY STATE	
CERTIFICATION OF COURT ACTION BY COUNTY CLERK	34A DATE OF ENTRY OF THE INTERLOCUTORY DECREE IF ANY	34B TYPE OF DECREE OR OTHER DISPOSITION (SPECIFY DISSOLUTION OF MARRIAGE JUDGMENT OF NULLITY LEGAL SEPARATION OR DISMISSAL)	34C DATE ENTERED
	I hereby certify that a judgment has been entered granting the type of decree specified in item 34.	35 COUNTY CLERK ▶	36 BY ▶ DEPUTY

STATE OF CALIFORNIA
DEPARTMENT OF PUBLIC HEALTH   TRIP OR CHP   BUREAU OF VITAL STATISTICS REGISTRATION
(REV 1-1 70) FORM VS-243A

You and Real Estate Law

Often you are the first person contacted by the real estate broker or client, and you can start the transaction off. If a broker is involved, request a copy of the contract between the buyer and seller and an abstract of title, or ascertain if title insurance is to be used.

If there is no broker involved, make an appointment for the client to come in to see the attorney so that the attorney can prepare a contract to buy and sell.

When the Client Is Selling Real Estate

The first step when the attorney represents the seller of real estate is to bring the abstract to date, if an abstract is available. If you type the abstract continuation, first type a caption sheet which shows the period the continuation covers and the legal description of the real estate.

FIGURE 8-1

Caption Sheet for Abstract Continuation

BLACK & JONES
Attorneys at Law
330 Main Street
Anytown, U.S.A.

CONTINUATION OF

ABSTRACT OF TITLE

From   To

For the following real estate:

Situated in the State of Ohio, in the County of Franklin, and in the City of Columbus:

> Being Lot No. One Hundred Forty (140) in the HILLSDALE SUBDIVISION to the City of Columbus, as the same is numbered and delineated upon the recorded plat thereof, of record in Plat Book No. 1400, page 1, Recorder's Office, Franklin County, Ohio.

Starting on a new sheet (8½x14), continue with the sections beginning with Section 1, placing two sections to a page. Number each section consecutively.

Following are various forms which might make up the sections of an abstract continuation. They will vary with each abstract. One abstract might contain abstracts of an estate, or even two estates; another might contain just a warranty deed, a mortgage, and a mortgage cancellation; another might contain a divorce, a marriage, a civil suit, or a lien against the property.

FIGURE 8-2

```
                                WARRANTY DEED
(Names of Grantors              Signed_____, 19___
and marital status)             Filed _____, 19___
                                Consideration $1.00 etc.
        to                      Two Witnesses
                                Transfer Tax
(Names of grantees)             Deed Book_____, Page _____
```

Grant, bargain, sell and convey to grantees, their heirs and assigns forever.

Premises described at the title page of this continuation.

Subject to conditions, restrictions, reservations, easements, if any, contained in former instruments of record.

To have and to hold the same to said grantees, their heirs and assigns forever.

Covenants of seizin and warranty, free and clear, except
taxes and assessments due_____

Special release of dower by wife.

_____, 19_____, acknowledged by grantors,
before _____, Notary Public, _____
County (State of) _____, Seal.

FIGURE 8-3

(Names and marital status   QUIT-CLAIM DEED
   of grantors)   Signed _____, 19____
                                   Filed_____, 19___
        to   Consideration $1.00 etc.
                                   Two witnesses
(Names of grantees)   Deed Book_____, Page _____

Remise, release and forever quitclaim to grantee,
their heirs and assigns forever.

Premises described at the title page of this continuation.

To have and to hold the same to said grantees, their
heirs and assigns forever.

Special release of dower by wife.

_____, 19_____, acknowledged by grantors
before _____, Notary Public, _____
County (State of _____, Seal.

FIGURE 8-4

```
(Names and marital status     MORTGAGE FOR $
   of grantors)               Premises described at the
                              caption of this continuation
      to                      (title page)
                              Signed                , 19
(Name of grantee)             Filed                 , 19
                              Two witnesses
                              M. R.          Page
```

Given to secure mortgagors' promissory note of even

date for the sum of $, payable with interest as

provided for in said note.

_____, 19____, acknowledged by mortgagors

before _____, Notary Public, _____County,

State of _____, seal.

NOT SATISFIED OF RECORD

FIGURE 8-5

The following memorandum appears on the margin of the

record of the above Mortgage recorded in M. R.   ,

Page

"The conditions of the within mortgage having been
complied with the same is hereby cancelled and
discharged this   day of   , 19 .
(by order of the Board of Directors.)

                    (Name of Mortgagee)

                    By_____

                    Attest_____

Copied from the original mortgage_____.

                    (Name of County Recorder)

                    By_____, Deputy Recorder.
```
```

FIGURE 8-6

(Names of First Parties)   LAND CONTRACT
                                  Signed _____
    to   Filed_____
                                  Two witnesses
(Names of Second Parties)   Misc. Record Vol._____, Page____

    On premises described at the title page of this
continuation.

    Purchase price of $_____, $_____cash paid down
and balance payable in monthly installments of $_____,
commencing _____and thereafter, _____per cent rate
of interest.

    Second party agrees to pay all taxes and assessments
beginning with _____collection.

    Recites mortgage to _____
which parties of the first part are to keep in good standing.

    Signed by _____and _____,
parties of the first part, and _____and
_____,parties of the second part, before
_____, Notary Public, State of _____,
_____19_____.   Seal.

                NOT CANCELLED OF RECORD

FIGURE 8-7

SECTION _____

        ESTATE OF _____

     The Probate Court records, Franklin County, Ohio,

Case No. _____, Administration Docket No._____,

Page_____, shows that _____died

_____, 19_____, that on _____, 19____,

_____was appointed Administrator (rix)

Executor (rix) and on:

(Dates)_____Bond dispensed by Will.

_____Entry approving bond and granting Letters of
        Authority filed.

_____Will admitted to Probate and Record
        C.D._____, page _____.

_____Application for and Entry appointing appraisers filed.

_____Notice of appointment and proof of publication filed.

_____Inventory and Appraisement filed, Personal $_____;
        Real Estate $_____.

_____Copy of Preliminary Notice given.

_____Entry ordering hearing on Inventory filed.

_____Application to Determine Inheritance Tax filed
        C. D._____, page _____.

_____Proof of publication of Notice and Entry
        approving Inventory filed.

_____Schedule of Debts filed.

_____Receipt of payment of Inheritance Tax filed.

_____Application for, consent to, and Entry ordering
        distribution in kind.

_____Final and Distributive Account filed and suspended
        for hearing.

_____Application for and Entry authorizing transfer
        of real estate filed and certificate issued.

ESTATE OF _____(Continued)

_____Entry ordering publication of Account filed.

_____Proof of publication of Account filed.

_____Account confirmed, estate settled, fiduciary and
bondsmen discharged.

_____Application for Entry allowing Attorney's fees
filed.

SECTION _____

THE HEIRS OF _____

The Probate Court records, Franklin County, Ohio,

Case No. _____, Will Record_____, Page _____,

shows by the sworn statement of _____that

_____died (in)testate in the _____

of _____, Franklin County, Ohio, leaving

_____, surviving spouse, and the following

next of kin:

Name	Address	Relationship

SECTION _____

The Probate Court records., Franklin County, Ohio, Case

No. _____, C.D._____, page _____, W.R._____,

page _____, shows that on _____, 19_____,

"Waiver of Notice and Consent to Probate" was filed, signed

by _____, _____, _____.

(Continued)

SECTION _____

       (insert Will)   double space
       2 sections per page or use
       Xerox copy of original will

Filed _____, 19_____

Wi_ Record_____, page_____   Two witnesses.

                          CLOSED

                       (OR PENDING)

SECTION _____

In the matter of   Certificate of Transfer
The Estate of   Probate Court, Franklin
                                    County, Ohio, Case No._____
_____, deceased   Signed   19
                                    Filed   19
                                    Deed Book   , page

        This is to certify that _____
died (in)testate on the _____day of _____, 19____;
that his place of residence at death was _____
and that the following is a description of each parcel of
real estate situated in Ohio owned by decedent at the time
of death.

        Premises described at caption of this Continuation.

        That such real estate passed (under his or her Will)
(by the laws of intestate succession) to the following:

Name   Age   Address   Relationship   Interest

Record of Will is in Will Record_____, page_____.
Record of administration is in Administration Docket____
page_____.

                          /s/_____
                                    Judge
                          By_____
                                          Deputy Clerk

TAIL SHEET

When the sections are all completed the continuation is concluded with a tail sheet which also contains numbered sections. Often the tail sheet is preprinted as it contains certain standard items that the abstracter does or does not check. Number the sections and fill in the appropriate blanks, usually information concerning taxes, parcel number, lot number, how title stands in the auditor's office, and the number of sections in the continuation. The tail sheet also contains the signature of the abstracter.

Use a numbering system and show the number assigned to the continuation on the tail sheet (described in Chapter 5). Also, be certain that the tail sheet is signed by the abstracter, or it may be more convenient to have the abstracter sign a number of tail sheets in advance.

FIGURE 8-8

Tail Sheet

SECTION
No old age pension liens, unsatisfied mechanics' liens, unexpired leases, land contracts, or miscellaneous matters of record upon said premises unless noted.

SECTION
No unsatisfied foreign executions in the Office of the Sheriff of Franklin County, Ohio, unless noted.

SECTION
No unsatisfied judgments, pending suits or Certificates of Judgment in the Court of Common Pleas or Court of Appeals affecting the premises unless noted.

SECTION
No unsatisfied Federal Tax Liens, unsatisfied Personal Tax Liens, or Unemployment Compensation Liens against said premises unless noted.

SECTION
No unsatisfied Recognizance Liens, notations on Notice Index, pursuant to Ohio Revised Code Sections 5301.47, *et seq.* or Financing Statements against or affecting said premises unless noted.

SECTION

The premises are shown on the Franklin County Auditor's Transfer Records, in the name of: _____ at a valuation of:

LAND $ BUILDINGS $ Total $

Parcel No. as to: (Lot No.)

Shown as: (Street address)

SECTION

The Taxes for

SECTION

Special taxes noted on the Treasurer's Duplicate: (No examination made for assessments not indexed or otherwise shown on the County Treasurer's Duplicate).

No examination made in any United States Court, nor in any United States Marshall's Office, nor for chattel mortgages or conditional sales contracts.

I hereby certify that the foregoing continuation of Abstract of Title, consisting of   Sections was collated by me from the records of Franklin County, Ohio, and I believe the same contains all matters of record in said County affecting the premises described at the title page hereof, as shown by the indexes to said records.

Respectfully submitted,

_____

Attorney at law

Columbus, Ohio

Dated:

No.

ADDENDA

On occasion an addendum to an abstract continuation is required. This is often requested by the buyer's attorney for some special reason, usually that something has been omitted from the abstract. An addendum should be ignored when dating a continuation as it does not usually cover a certain period, but one item.

FIGURE 8-9

A D D E N D A

To the foregoing abstract of title:

   (Description of property)

This addenda is being made at the request of_____.

SECTION_____

    I hereby certify that I have collated the above

addenda consisting of one section from the Recorder's

Office, Franklin County, Ohio.

                Respectfully submitted,

                By_____
                    Attorney at law

Columbus, Ohio
Date

NO-CHANGE CERTIFICATE

On occasion a no-change certificate is required, usually when the abstract is "stale" (too old). The no-change certificate merely certifies that there have been no changes in the courthouse records since the date of the last continuation.

FIGURE 8-10

No-Change Certificate

Columbus, Ohio (Date)

I hereby certify that there are no changes of record affecting the foregoing abstract of title of the following premises:

(describe real estate)

since the date of the last continuation made by me dated _____ to date.

Respectfully submitted,

BLACK & JONES

By _____
       Homer J. Black

TITLE INSURANCE

If an abstract is not available, title insurance may be used. If the seller was furnished title insurance when he himself purchased the property, it is best to order a reissue of his policy in the same company, as the premium is less on a reissue. You can obtain the policy number from the previous policy and order the title insurance. Order a copy of the preliminary binder sent to the buyer's attorney, and to any loaning institution the purchaser is using, as well as a copy sent to your attorney.

DRAWING THE DEED

When the abstract is continued or the title binder has been received, you are ready to draw the deed. There are many forms of deeds available at your stationers. You will find forms for Warranty Deeds, Quit-claim Deeds, deed from a corporation to an individual, deeds from an individual to a corporation, deeds from a corporation to a corporation, deeds used in estates such as administrator's or executor's deeds, deeds under the authority of the will (to be used when the real estate is sold according to the terms of a Will), or a short form statutory deed for administrators and executors (such as is currently used by Ohio).

First determine which type of deed to use. To do this you will have to ascertain who the sellers and buyers are. If the seller is an individual and he is selling to a corporation, use a deed from an individual to a corporation; if the seller is an administrator of an estate, use an administrator's or executor's deed; if the seller is an individual selling to an individual use a general warranty deed (some states have authorized the use of a short-form, one-page statutory warranty deed which saves considerable typing) (Figure 8-11). Whether you use a long or short form warranty deed usually depends on the length of the description.

The statutory deed may be used in place of the usual Warranty Deed and eliminates much repetition of phrases in the general warranty deed.

After determining the type of deed required, determine in whose name the title stands. To do this, turn to the back of the abstract and, leafing through it backwards, locate the last transfer wherein the present owner took title. The last transfer might be a warranty deed, a quit-claim deed, a certificate of transfer in an estate, an administrator's or executor's deed, a commissioner's deed, or a sheriff's deed. The present owner might have taken title to one-half of the real estate at one time and one-half at a later date (i.e., on the death of a spouse). Note how the name of the owner reads (i.e., in one name or two), how it is spelled, etc. and show it the same way on your new deed as grantor. If you find a discrepancy of spelling in the abstract, say James C. Brown on the deed and James Charles Brown on the mortgage you should show the grantor on your deed as James C. Brown aka James Charles Brown. If your state has dower laws the grantor would read: James C. Brown aka James Charles Brown and Mary Brown, his wife. If title is in both husband's and wife's names, your grantor would read: James C. Brown aka James Charles Brown and Mary Brown, husband and wife.

Ascertain the grantee or buyer's name or names from the contract

FIGURE 8-11

GENERAL WARRANTY DEED
SECTIONS 5302.05 and 5302.06, Ohio Revised Code

of

County   for valuable consideration paid, grant

with general warranty covenants, to

whose tax mailing address is

the following Real Property:

Situated in the County of   in the State of Ohio, and in the

of

This deed is executed and delivered by Grantor and accepted by Grantee(s) subject to all legal highways and subject to, and with the benefit of all restrictions, easements, conditions, limitations and reservations of record, if any, and to zoning restrictions which have been imposed thereon, if any.

Free and clear from all incumbrances whatsoever, excepting taxes and assessments due at the collection and thereafter.

Prior Deed Reference: D.B.   Page

Grantor(s) release all respective rights of dower therein.

Witness   hand(s) this   day of   , 197

SIGNED AND ACKNOWLEDGED IN THE PRESENCE OF:

_____
Witness

_____
Witness

State of   ,   County, SS:

BE IT REMEMBERED that on this   day of   , 197   , before me, the subscriber, a Notary Public, in and for said County, personally came

the Grantor(s) in the foregoing deed and acknowledged the signing thereof to be voluntary act and deed.

IN TESTIMONY WHEREOF, I have hereunto subscribed my name and affixed my official seal on this day and year as aforesaid.

_____
NOTARY PUBLIC

and insert on the deed, and add the legal description (from caption sheet of abstract or from title binder).

The record of the volume and page number in which the last transfer was recorded at the court house should also be added to the deed in the appropriate place (usually after the legal description).

MORTGAGE ASSUMPTION CLAUSE

If the current mortgage is being assumed by the buyer, include a mortgage assumption clause in the deed, usually after the "Exception" clause as follows:

> Excepting a mortgage in the original amount of $16,000, dated August 23, 19———, and given by grantors to Hattwell Mortgage Company, said mortgage being recorded in M.R. 2279, page 500, Recorder's Office, Franklin County, Ohio, which the grantees assume and agree to pay as part of the consideration for this transfer.

RESERVING LIFE ESTATE

On occasion a parent or other person may wish to transfer a piece of real estate to his children, or others, but reserve for himself the right to live in the house as long as he lives. Following is an example of a clause reserving a life estate, which can be inserted in a warranty deed to cover such a situation:

> EXCEPTING AND RESERVING to the grantor, Iva T. Smith, and her assigns, an estate in the above-described premises for and during the natural life of said grantor.

Type this clause after the legal description, and then in the Habendum Clause starting "To Have and to Hold" and after "her heirs and assigns forever" type "after the death of the grantor." Or, on a statutory deed, type it after the grantees' names.

LAND CONTRACT CLAUSE

When the real estate has been sold on land contract and the purchase price is paid in full, a warranty deed should be given to the purchaser with the following clause inserted after the legal description:

This conveyance is executed and delivered by the grantors and
accepted by the grantees as compliance in full with the terms of a
land contract entered into between the parties hereto on March 2,
19——, said land contract being recorded in Mortgage Record 2493,
page 370, Recorder's Office, Franklin County, Ohio.

JOINT AND SURVIVORSHIP CLAUSE

Some persons prefer to take title to a piece of property by joint
and survivorship. In this case use the following clause after the
grantee's name:

William H. Boggs and Jean Boggs, during their joint lives, and the
remainder to the survivor of them, his or her separate heirs and
assigns.

SIGNATURES

Each grantor should sign the deed and each grantor's name should
be typewritten beneath a line at the end of the deed.

ACKNOWLEDGEMENT

Each grantor must have his signature acknowledged before a
notary public and each name should be typed in the acknowledgement clause.

TITLE INSURANCE

If title insurance is used, check the title binder to see who holds
the fee simple to the property and type these names as grantor on
the new deed.

When the Client is Purchasing Real Estate

When the client is buying real estate you cannot be as useful. The
attorney must make the title search and dictate a title opinion.
However, title opinions can be partially taken from the form book
with certain parts dictated. The following title opinion is a sample
that you can keep in the form book and adapt to each case:

FIGURE 8-12

Title Opinion

January 1, 19_____

(Name and Address of Client)

Dear Mr. and Mrs._____

I have examined the abstract of title for the following described premises situated in the State of Ohio, County of Franklin, and in the City of_____, and bounded and described as follows:

> (here copy legal description of
> real estate from abstract or
> title binder)

Assuming the correctness of the abstract, the last continuation having been made by_____, and dated _____, title is in the name of_____, who obtained title by deed recorded in Deed Book Volume _____ , page _____ , subject to the following comments and encumbrances:

1. There are small defects in the early part of the abstract which have been cured by time and, in my opinion, do not affect the title.

2. Lot No. 24 is irregular in shape and is located on the northwest side of Polly Drive. It has a frontage of 75 feet on Polly Drive. The depth on the northeast line is 183.08 feet; on the southwest line the depth is 191 feet; the rear of the lot is irregular, starting at the northeast corner it runs in a southwesterly direction 65.60 feet to a point and then at an angle 42 feet to the southwest corner of the lot. It has a 50-foot setback line from Polly Drive from the northeast corner with a 48-foot building setback line on the south line. There is a 25-foot easement at the rear of the lot for utility purposes.

3. The restrictions are set forth in a deed found in D.B. 2216, page 424. This deed is shown in Section 108 of the abstract. The restrictions are very extensive, and I will not set them forth in this opinion. They require a residence only and are to your advantage, but I would suggest that you check these restrictions carefully with your contractor before plans are drawn to build.

4. There is a mortgage given by_____ to The Grabiel Mortgage Company in the original amount of $18,000, recorded in M.R. Volume_____, page_____, which is a lien on the premises.

5. The property is listed on the tax duplicate as land only and no valuation has been assigned as yet to it. Taxes for the year 19_____ in the amount of $, the first half of which are due in the December, 19_____, collection, are unpaid and a lien. Taxes for the year 19_____ are undetermined. The property is listed as Parcel No._____, and the street address is shown as_____

6. You should satisfy yourself that there are no unrecorded land contracts, leases, mechanics' liens or easements affecting this lot. You should consider the rights of parties now in possession of the premises, and also satisfy yourself as to whether there are any encroachments affecting them. An affidavit should be obtained at the time of closing that all bills for labor and materials have been paid.

Subject to the above, a warranty deed from_____ and _____, with proper release of dower, should convey to you a good and merchantable title in said premises. You should also execute BTA Form No. 100 prescribed by the Ohio Department of Taxation and see to it that the amount of $_____is withheld from the sellers in order to pay the conveyance fee in the Franklin County Auditor's Office.

Respectfully submitted,

BLACK AND JONES

By

John P. Black

JPB: bt

In addition, you can prepare a seller's affidavit which the seller signs and which guarantees to the buyer that no work has been done on the house that is not paid for and therefore, no mechanics' liens will be filed against the property.

FIGURE 8-13

BLACK & JONES
Attorneys at Law
30 Main Street
Anywhere, U.S.A.

AFFIDAVIT

STATE OF OHIO
FRANKLIN COUNTY, SS:

_____and _____being first
duly sworn depose(s) and state(s) that they are (he is) this
day conveying and selling the following described real estate:

(describe real estate)

The undersigned say there are no liens or encumbrances on
said premises excepting such as are shown by the abstract of
title or title policy which has been submitted for examination;
that no liens have been given or created by the undersigned,
or acquired by any person on said premises since the date of
the last continuation of said abstract or title policy; that
the undersigned knows of no existing defect in title to said
premises; that no question regarding the same has ever been
raised by anyone whomsoever to the knowledge of this affiant;
that the buildings, if any, on said premises are located within
the lot lines thereof and there are no structural defects
therein to the knowledge of this affiant; that no labor or
materials have been furnished for the repair or improvement
of said premises during the past sixty days and not paid for;
that there has been no change in the marital status of the
undersigned during the period of ownership of said premises
which would in any way affect the title that has not been
reported to the proposed purchaser thereof; that there are no
encroachments upon the property to the knowledge of this affiant;
that the occupying tenants, if any, have no claim on said
property other than as month-to-month tenants; and that this
affidavit is made for the purpose of inducing the purchaser
to buy and pay for said premises, and the loan company, or
other third person, to grant a loan or extend credit thereon.

The undersigned knows of no omission or mistake in the
abstract to said property which would affect the title to
said premises, which has not been called to the attention of
the proposed purchaser and to the loan company.

Further affiant saith not.

_____

_____

Sworn to before me and subscribed in my presence this
day of   , 19   .

_____
NOTARY PUBLIC

Preparing the Closing Statements

While the attorney probably will work out the actual figures for the closing statement, it will be helpful to him if you verify his figures on your adding machine to detect any arithmetic errors and after it is typed, to detect typing errors in the figures.

Make up and duplicate a work sheet for buyer's and seller's statements and keep it in the form file for future use.

FIGURE 8-14

Seller's Statement of Real Estate Closing

DATE OF CLOSING:
PROPERTY:
SELLERS:
BUYERS:
REAL ESTATE BROKER:
ATTORNEY FOR BUYERS:
ATTORNEY FOR SELLERS:
PLACE OF CLOSING:

—————————————————

Sale Price $———

Less charges to sellers:

  Real Estate Taxes prorated to date $———

  Transfer Tax   ———

  Mortgage payoff balance   ———

  Mortgage cancellation fee   ———

  Termite inspection report   ———

  Real Estate Commission   ———

  Legal expense   ———

  Additional charges   ———

                                                        ———

                                                        ———

    Total charges to sellers   ———

    Net to seller   ———

FIGURE 8-15

Work Sheet for Buyers' Closing Statement

```
DATE OF CLOSING:
PROPERTY:
SELLERS:
BUYERS:
REAL ESTATE BROKER:
ATTORNEY FOR BUYERS:
ATTORNEY FOR SELLERS:
PLACE OF CLOSING:
```

Purchase Price $_____

Additional charges to buyer:

    Loan Service Charge $_____

    Recording & Transfer charges   _____

    Interest on Mortgage to_____   _____

    Re-continue abstract   _____

    Payments into escrow   _____

    _____   _____

    _____   _____

    Legal   _____

                                           $

Credits to buyer:

    Real Estate Taxes:

        Last half 1971   _____

        1972 prorated to
            date   _____   _____ $_____

Paid as follows: $_____

If the closing statement is prepared ahead of or during the closing, it is good practice to place the word "Approved" at the bottom of the statement and place signature lines for the buyer and seller. If the closing statement is made up after the closing, this can be omitted. Unless the attorney deducts his fee at the closing, the closing statement made up beforehand will not reflect the client's complete tax basis in the property for income tax purposes. The tax lawyer who also handles real estate transactions and is, therefore, conscious of tax savings, may wish to advise his client as to his complete tax basis so that when his income tax return is made up, the preparer will have all the necessary information at hand. The attorney in this case may send a second closing statement and a special letter giving tax advice, along with his billing, after the closing.

FIGURE 8-16

Final Buyers' Statement of Real Estate Closing

```
DATE OF CLOSING:  January 25, 19__
PROPERTY:   60 - 64 Park Street, Anywhere, U. S. A.
SELLERS:  Clinton A. and Elizabeth M. Parrott
BUYERS:   Charles B. and Bonnie M. Green
REAL ESTATE BROKERS:  Sharp Realty Co.
ATTORNEY FOR BUYERS:  John J. Black
ATTORNEY FOR SELLERS:  Carl O. O'Malley
```

Purchase Price		$ 14,500.00
Additional charges to buyer:		
Recording and Transfer charges	$ 4.46	
Legal	85.00	89.46
		$ 14,589.46
Credits to buyers:		
Real Estate taxes prorated to date	$ 79.37	
Rental adjustment	23.87	103.24
		$ 14,486.22

FIGURE 8-17

Letter to a Client Who Has Sold and Bought a Residence

BLACK & JONES
Attorneys at Law
30 Main Street
Anywhere, U. S. A.

January 1, 19__

Mr. and Mrs. Gordon D. Schmidt
1202 High Street
Anywhere, U. S. A.

In re purchase of 1202 High Street

Dear Mr. and Mrs. Schmidt:

Enclosed find buyers' statement of real estate closing
which differs somewhat from the one you received at
the closing as it reflects your end only of the transaction in which you purchased the above-mentioned real
estate, and all of your charges are reflected in it.

I would suggest that you show this statement to whoever
prepares your 19__ Federal income tax return as it will
be necessary for you to file a Federal form showing the
sale of your old residence and purchase of your new one,
and the statement will be helpful at that time.

I would also suggest that you keep a close record of
all the capital improvements you make on your new residence such as shrubbery, remodeling, furnaces, fences,
air conditioners, etc. as this will increase your basis
and may save you income tax in the event you sell at a
gain.

May I thank you for allowing me to represent you in this
matter, and if you have any questions about it at any time,
feel free to call me.

Very truly yours,

BLACK & JONES

John D. Black

JDB:bt
Enclosures

FIGURE 8-18

Letter to Client Who Has Purchased a Residence

BLACK & JONES
Attorneys at Law
30 Main Street
Anywhere, U.S.A.

January 1, 19_____

Mr. and Mrs. Frank S. Matson
123 Park Street
Anywhere, U.S.A.

In re Purchase of 123 Park Street

Dear Mr. and Mrs. Matson:

Enclosed find buyers' statement of real estate closing, which
differs somewhat from the one you received at the closing as it
reflects your end only of the transaction in which you purchased the
above-mentioned real estate and all of your charges are reflected
in it.

I would suggest that you keep this statement as it reflects your
original basis in the property for income tax purposes.

I would also suggest that you keep close records of all permanent
improvements you make on the property such as fences, landscaping,
furnaces, air conditioners, new roof, remodelling, etc. as these
expenditures will increase your tax basis and will save taxes in the
event you sell the property at a gain.

May I thank you for allowing me to represent you in this matter.
If you have any questions, please call me.

Very truly yours,
BLACK & JONES

John D. Black

JDB:bt
Enclosure

When You Set Up the Closing

When the closing is held in the attorney's office (usually when there is no bank loan being obtained) the buyer should have his choice of location of closing. You may be called upon to telephone each of the parties involved—the buyer, the seller, the attorney for the buyer or seller other than your lawyer, and the broker—and arrange a time suitable to all.

On these occasions funds may have to be disbursed through the law office trust account, and the attorney may wish you to prepare a statement of funds disbursed through his trust account, and the statement distributed to all interested parties. It should read as follows:

August 1, 19_____

STATEMENT OF FUNDS RECEIVED AND DISBURSED
THROUGH BUTLER AND JONES TRUST ACCOUNT

Miller-Parks Transaction

Placed into trust account by buyer		$10,000.00
Disbursed as follows:		
Hartwell Mortgage Co.		
mortgage payoff	$8,000.00	
Mortgage cancellation fee	1.00	
Transfer tax	15.00	
Title Insurance	100.00	
Termite report	10.00	
Carl & Mary Miller	1,874.00	$10.000.00

Approved: Approved:

_____   _____

Carl Miller   Harold D. Parks

_____   _____

Mary Miller   Phyllis O. Parks

        SELLERS   BUYERS

Total all disbursements on your adding machine to make certain they equal the amount to be placed into the trust account, issue the checks, total them to verify the amount, and make the necessary records on a 3x5 card for the trust account file. (How to keep records of trust monies is discussed in Chapter Four.)

Whether your attorney represents the buyer or the seller he may wish to obtain an amortization schedule for his client's mortgage which shows monthly balance. For two copies send one dollar to the Financial Publishing Company, 82 Brookline Avenue, Boston, Massachusetts 02115. Give amount of loan, interest rate, and how payable, term of loan, and monthly payment.

You and Trial Law

Some lawyers prefer a separate file for all trial work, thus facilitating the location of trial files.

Keeping the Lawyer's Calendar

As the cases are assigned, mark them on the lawyer's calendar so that he will put in his appearance at the proper time and place and have time to prepare pleadings. Jot down the name of the client and the name of the court in which the trial is to take place. Also note if the case is up for pretrial or trial.

FIGURE 9-1

TRIAL DOCKET
Week of 1-1-

Lawyers

Style of the Case	Black	Burns	Gorman
State vs. Cobb, No. 162804 Court of Appeals Criminal	1-4 9:30 a.m.		
Green vs. Wittaker No. 17509 Common Pleas Personal Injury suit			1-6 10:00 a.m.

Style of the Case	Black	Burns	Gorman
Jenkins vs. Brown et al No. 17512 Common Pleas Will Contest		1-5 2:00 p.m.	
Ludwig vs. Camden No. 17520 Common Pleas Personal Injury			1-5 2:30 a.m.
State vs. Krakoff No. 17456 Supreme Court Criminal	1-4 11:00 a.m.		

You may find it is your job to maintain trial docket for more than one lawyer. In this case, get the trials on each lawyer's calendar as they are assigned. In addition, make up a trial list once a week, listing each lawyer, and noting each case he has assigned that week by style of case and your office file number, if one has been assigned. Changes that come in during the week can be written in.

The underlined names in the style of the case indicate the client.

Preparing the Pleadings

There are many different reasons why people go into court and bring suits against others, but in this chapter we will look at pleadings for (1) personal injury suits arising out of automobile accidents; and (2) criminal proceedings in defense of a person who has committed a crime.

PERSONAL INJURY SUITS ARISING OUT OF AUTOMOBILE ACCIDENTS

The suit arising out of an automobile accident must be filed within a specified time, usually set by statute in your state. The New England states are piloting the "no-fault" insurance claim which, if adopted by other states, will eliminate the personal injury suit; but until such time people will, no doubt, continue to file personal injury suits arising out of automobile accidents.

Following is a sample complaint which is the first pleading to be prepared. In the sample, both husband and wife were involved in the accident and each prays for damages against the defendants.

FIGURE 9-2

IN THE COURT OF COMMON PLEAS, FRANKLIN COUNTY, OHIO

James and Wyvonnie Cochran :
1029 Bancroft Road
Columbus, Ohio 43229 :

Plaintiffs :

vs. : Case No.
25,000

Nancy L. Brown :
1099 Fisher Road
Columbus, Ohio 43206 :

Dale M. Brown :
1099 Fisher Road
Columbus, Ohio 43206 :

Defendants :

COMPLAINT

First Claim

(1) On November 19, 19_____, at the intersection of the public streets called Cleveland Avenue and East North Broadway in Columbus, Ohio, the defendant, Nancy L. Brown, negligently drove her car, which was owned by the defendant, Dale M. Brown, into the car being driven by the Plaintiff, Wyvonnie Cochran.

(2) As a result, Wyvonnie Cochran suffered ligamentous injury to the cervical spine, contusions and soreness about her face, head and neck and injuries to her veins, arteries and nerves.

(3) Wyvonnie Cochran has incurred permanent damages, pain and suffering and expects to incur further pain and suffering in the future.

(4) Wyvonnie Cochran has suffered loss of wages, and, because her husband, Lawrence, was also involved in this accident and experienced personal injury as a result, she has lost the services and consortium of her husband in the past and will suffer further loss of services and consortium in the future.

Second Claim

(1)   For a Second Claim, Plaintiff, James Cochran, incorporates the allegations of the first three paragraphs of the First Claim herein.

(2)   Plaintiff, James Cochran, is the husband of Wyvonnie Cochran and was a passenger in the automobile being driven by his wife which was struck by the automobile that was negligently driven by the defendant, Nancy L. Brown.

(3)   As a result of this accident, James Cochran suffered ligamentous injury to the cervical spine, contusions and soreness about his face, head, neck and injury to his veins, arteries and nerves.

(4)   As a result of this accident, James Cochran has incurred damage, pain and suffering and expects to incur further pain and suffering in the future.

(5)   Also as a result of this accident, James Cochran has incurred medical and hospital expenses for his wife and himself in the amount of $1,594.77, and expects to incur further such expenses in the future.

(6)   As a result of this accident, the Plaintiffs have suffered lost wages in the amount of $643.36 and expect to incur further lost wages in the future.

(7)   As a further result of this accident, the Plaintiffs have incurred expenses for car rental and cab fare in the amount of $132.15.

(8)   As a further result of this accident, the Plaintiff, James Cochran, has lost the services and consortium of his wife in the past and will suffer further loss of services and consortium in the future.

WHEREFORE, Plaintiff, Wyvonnie Cochran prays for damages against defendants in the sum of Forty Thousand Dollars ($40,000.00), and the Plaintiff, James Cochran, prays for damages against the defendants in the sum of Twenty-Five Thousand Dollars ($25,000.00) and costs.

James O. Brown
BROWN & HORN
Attorneys at Law
330 Main Street
Any Town, U.S.A.

In this sample case, it was deemed advisable to file interrogatories, a set of questions which the party requested must answer. Following are the interrogatories filed in the sample case.

FIGURE 9-3

IN THE COURT OF COMMON PLEAS, FRANKLIN COUNTY, OHIO

James and Wyvonnie Cochran

    Plaintiffs

   vs.

Nancy L. Brown
Dale M. Brown

    Defendants

Case No. 25,000

INTERROGATORIES

Pursuant to the provisions of Civil Rule 33, the defendant Nancy L. Brown, is required to answer the following Interrogatories fully, in writing, and under oath.

1. State:

    a. Your name.
    b. Your address.
    c. Your date of birth.

2. State the date, time and place of the accident.

3. State the name and address of the owner of said vehicle at the time of the occurrence.

4. State in detail how the alleged accident occurred.

5. State whether the motor vehicle owned by the defendant left any skid marks in the roadway as a result of this accident.

6. If the answer to the Interrogatory 5 is in the affirmative, then set forth:

    a. The length of such skid marks;
    b. In what lane of traffic and on what part of the roadway said skid marks existed.

7. State what the weather conditions were at the time and place of the accident.

8. State what the composition of the roadway was at the time and place of the accident.

9. Set forth the number of lanes of traffic there were at the place of the accident; whether any

lanes were separated from one another by lines or
marks and, if so, indicate in what manner said
lanes were separated.

10. State in what direction the defendant was travel-
ing immediately before the occurrence.

11. State whether there was any curve in the roadway
at the place of the accident.

12. If it is claimed that the vehicles came in contact
with each other, set forth:

    a. What part of the Plaintiff's vehicle was
involved in the impact, and

    b. What part of the defendant's vehicle was
involved in the impact.

13. State whether or not the defendant or any of her
representatives have made out any reports in
connection with this accident.

14. If the answer to the question immediately above
is, "yes":

    a. State to whom these reports were made.

    b. If she will do so without a Motion to Produce,
attach a copy of the report to the answers
to these Interrogatories.

15. State where the defendant had been coming from
and what her destination was.

16. State the purpose of the trip.

17. State when the defendant left her last previous
stop and the time she had to appear at this
destination.

18. State whether the defendant claims the Plaintiff
was guilty of any negligence in connection with
this accident.

19. If the answer to Interrogatory 18 is in the
affirmative, then state precisely in what respect
the defendant claims that the Plaintiff was
guilty of negligence.

20. State whether the defendant claims that the
Plaintiff violated any statute, ordinance, rule or
regulation in connection with the accident.

21. State whether the defendant was insured.

22. If the answer to the question immediately above is, "yes," state:

    a. The name of the insurance company.

    b. The amount of the policy limits.

Submitted by:

James O. Brown
BROWN & HORN
Attorneys at Law
330 Main Street
Any Town, U. S. A.

The defense attorney in a personal injury suit may wish to take the plaintiff's deposition. Much time in explaining this procedure to the client can be saved by preparing "Suggestions for Discovery Deposition." Make copies of these for use by the client when a deposition has been arranged.

Following is a sample.

FIGURE 9-4

Suggestions for Discovery Deposition

Under the law, the defense attorney has a right to take your "discovery deposition." This means that you will be put under oath, just as you would be in court, and the defense lawyer will ask you questions relating to this case. His questions and your answers will be taken down by a court reporter. One of your attorneys will be present at all times.

There will be no judge or jury present. However, after the deposition is over, the court reporter will type out all of the questions and answers, and both your attorney and the defense attorney will receive copies. The original will be filed in court.

If your case goes to trial and you are present, the only way this deposition can be used at the trial is in cross-examination of you by

the defense attorney if your testimony at trial should be any
different than your testimony at the time of the deposition.

For this reason, it is extremely important that you have everything in mind concerning the cause of your injuries and the nature
of your injuries at the time of the deposition. We will have an
opportunity to go over the matter with you before the deposition,
but it will be helpful if you will refresh your recollection before
you meet with us.

The defense attorney in this discovery deposition can ask you
questions that are admissible in court under the rules of the
evidence. In addition to this, he can also ask you questions that may
seem to you as if they are none of his business and that, actually,
under the rules of evidence, would not be admissible in court. However, the courts allow "discovery" in these depositions, and the
attorney may ask you for "hearsay" and other things that will
enable him to make further investigation of the case and further
preparation to defend it against you.

For this reason, do not be surprised if we do not object to
questions that seem to you to be out of line. If the defense
attorney questions you on any subject that is not proper on a
"discovery deposition," then we will object to the question. If we
object to the question and instruct you not to answer it, then you
should REFUSE TO ANSWER THE QUESTION. Please do not
refuse to answer any question that we have not instructed you to
refuse to answer.

Reasons for Taking This Deposition

It will assist the defendant and the defense attorney in evaluating
this case for settlement purposes. This is often the first and only
opportunity the defense attorney has to see the plaintiff before the
case comes to trial. Therefore, you should be clean and neatly
dressed; courteous and respectful to the defendant's attorneys and
all others in the room; be prepared to exhibit any injuries that might
be visible. You should answer the questions in an honest and straightforward manner, so the defense attorney will be impressed with the
fact that the jury will know, if the case is tried, that you are
completely honest and sincere.

The defense attorney will get all possible information regarding
names of witnesses, doctors, and items of that nature to assist him
in completing his investigation of the case and his preparation for
trial.

He will get you committed under oath to all of the facts concerning the cause of your injury and the nature and extent of your injuries, so that you cannot say anything different at the trial without being subject to impeachment with this deposition on cross-examination.

Probably, the most important reason for the deposition is to attempt to trap you into lying. One of the most effective ways to defend a case is to be able to prove that the plaintiff has lied in some way. Proving that you have lied under oath on a deposition is almost as effective as catching you in a lie in the courtroom.

How to Handle Yourself in the Deposition

We know that you would not deliberately lie, but it is important that you not be trapped into something that is not true. For this reason, LISTEN TO EACH QUESTION CAREFULLY AND BE SURE THAT YOU UNDERSTAND IT BEFORE ANSWERING. If you do not understand it, ask the defense attorney to repeat it or to rephrase it so you do understand it. When you understand the question, then answer it honestly and in a straightforward manner. If you do not know the answer, do not be afraid to say that you don't know or don't recall. No one can remember every minute detail. However, the important things you will remember and you should give an honest and full answer to questions on these points.

The defense attorney will probably be friendly and will not "bully" you in any manner. His theory will probably be that the more he can get you to say the more apt you are to get your "foot in your mouth." Therefore:

UNDERSTAND THE QUESTION. You don't have to hurry in answering.

ANSWER THAT QUESTION TRUTHFULLY.

STOP!

Do not volunteer anything. Give a full and complete answer to the question asked but do not anticipate any other question or attempt to answer it. If the defense attorney overlooks asking any questions he should ask, that is not your worry but his.

If the defense attorney should be rough in any manner, DO NOT LOSE YOUR TEMPER.

Speak loudly and clearly enough that everyone can hear and understand you.

Be careful of common traps:

Past Injuries: The defense attorney will undoubtedly ask you about injuries you have sustained in the past. At the time of the deposition—or at least before the trial—the defense attorney will have complete information from his investigation as to all past injuries that you have had of any kind, either on any job you have held, or in automobile wrecks or any other manner. Insurance companies and railroads have central index bureaus where they can get information on all injuries that persons have sustained; where they have been paid workmen's compensation, filed suit or recovered from any employer or insurance company, even health and accident insurance. Also, it is common for the defense in lawsuits to check on treatments you have had, medical doctors, osteopaths, chiropractors, and hospitals wherever you have lived and have been and in adjoining areas.

Therefore, as it is to every question asked, it is extremely important that you answer truthfully. Answer only the question you were asked here also. In other words, if you are asked what injuries you have had to the same part of your body that was injured this time, then limit your answer to that part of your body. Or, if you are asked what injuries you have had on a certain job or in automobile wrecks, then limit your answer to the question asked. If, however, you are asked generally about any injuries you have had, give the defense attorney the information requested as to any and all injuries of any type to any part of your body that you have had at any time. (This is something you should also be sure to tell us about before the deposition.)

Arrests and other lawsuits: Here, again, the defense already knows or will know before trial whether you have had any other lawsuits or ever have been arrested or the like. Even though it may be embarrassing, if you are asked this question, you should answer it truthfully. The embarrassment will have much less effect on your case than to be proven a liar or to be withholding information.

Activities since injury: Before the trial, perhaps before the deposition, the defense will have investigated what you do at work, at home, in your neighborhood, and any place else that you go. It is quite common for the defense to hire photographers to hide a block or so away, out of sight, and take movies with a telephoto lens of a person working around his house, on his job, or out fishing or engaged in activities of that nature.

As we have previously told you, fishing, mowing the lawn, working, or doing anything else you feel able to do (and that the doctor allows you to do) will not hurt you in and of itself. However, if you forget you have done something and say on your discovery deposition that you have not been able to do a certain thing, and the defense has movies or witnesses to prove that you have done that, then it will completely ruin your case.

Preparation for the Deposition

Refresh your recollection by reading any notes that you made after your injury, such as statements you have given or reports you have given or anything of that nature. If you have any additional medical or hospital bills or information on loss of earnings, or other damages that you have not yet given us, have it with you and give it to us before the deposition.

If it is practical, visit the scene of the injury and refresh your recollection concerning visibility, obstructions, distances, speeds, and the like.

You should not memorize any statement you have given or anything that you are going to say in answer to questions. You should simply visualize what happened and, in your own words, answer any questions concerning it.

General Rules

On questions asked you concerning your injuries and suffering, you do not have to "minimize" them; but, be extremely careful not to exaggerate the injuries or suffering.

As much as possible, stick to actual facts, rather than opinions as to times, distances, speeds, or the like. If it is necessary for you to give an opinion on such an item, then be careful to state that it is your own best estimate.

Please follow our recommendations at the deposition. You do not have to watch us as we will not "signal" you how to answer. However, sometimes the defense attorneys ask the client if he is willing to sign an authorization to allow the defense attorney to obtain medical reports or if he is willing to allow an examination by a doctor of the defendant's choosing. If something such as this is asked, you may simply state you will follow your lawyer's recommendation. Don't worry about remembering these questions; if they are asked we shall interrupt and ask you if you will follow our recommendation and you may simply say, "Yes."

In Conclusion

We hope these suggestions will help you. We realize it is easy to say "don't worry" but there is really nothing at all to fear. Get a good night's sleep before the deposition, tell the truth, and you will find that our chances of working out a fair settlement will be better after this deposition.

Sincerely,

BROWN & HORN

By

James O. Brown

There are other pleadings which may be filed in a personal injury suit, but we won't attempt to cover them all in this book. Make up often-used forms and keep them in your form book (discussed in Chapter Three).

CRIMINAL PROCEEDINGS IN DEFENSE OF A PERSON COMMITTING A CRIME

The following sample pleadings are taken from an actual case (fictitious name used) wherein a 21-year-old father was indicted and charged with first degree murder of his 3-month-old son. According to the defendant's story, he and his 17-year-old wife had an argument, and she left home. The defendant then put a .22-caliber, short-barrelled rifle to his head, contemplating suicide, but instead lowered the gun. The gun discharged as it was brought down, hitting the child in the forehead.

A request for clarification of the charge of first-degree murder was filed.

FIGURE 9-5

IN THE COURT OF COMMON PLEAS, FRANKLIN COUNTY, OHIO

State of Ohio   :

      Plaintiff-Appellee   :

vs.   ·   Case No.
35,000

Charles O. Forman   ·

      Defendant   :

Defendant's Request for Special Instructions on the Charge of First-Degree Murder

The Defendant requests that the Court charge, on the element of purpose and intent, as follows:

> Purpose and intent to kill must have existed in the mind of the accused for such period of time as to preclude the idea that the said purpose and intent to kill were formed for the first time at the very time of the act of killing.

The above-stated law was taken from *Twiman vs. State* (13 OL Abs, page 459).

      BROWN & HORN

      By‗‗‗‗‗‗‗‗‗‗‗‗

      James O. Brown
      Attorneys for Charles O. Forman,
      Defendant

The charge was reduced to second-degree murder, the defendant was found guilty, and a motion for a new trial was filed.

FIGURE 9-6

IN THE COURT OF COMMON PLEAS, FRANKLIN COUNTY, OHIO
CRIMINAL DIVISION

State of Ohio   :

        Plaintiff   :

vs.   :   Case No. 35,000

Charles O. Forman   :

        Defendant   :

MOTION FOR NEW TRIAL

Now comes Charles O. Forman, Defendant herein, and moves the Court for a new trial in this cause for the following reasons, to wit:

1. Irregularity in the proceedings of the Court by which the Defendant was prevented from having a fair trial.

2. Errors of law occurring at trial.

3. The verdict of "Guilty of Second Degree Murder" is not sustained by sufficient evidence and is contrary to law.

BROWN & HORN

By_____
James O. Brown
Attorneys for Defendant

Memorandum

Defendant states that the Court committed error by questioning the Venire, as a whole, on their attitude on capital punishment and refusing counsel for the Defendant additional opportunity to question the Veniremen individually in this matter. The effect of this error was to leave only those persons who had a predilection towards more harsh treatment of Defendants charged with "First Degree Murder."

Defendant further states that errors of law were committed by the Court in allowing to remain in evidence that part of the testimony of Police Officer Corder which pertained to powder burns and the distance between the decedent and the murder weapon. Defendant feels this testimony was inadmissible

because it was based on heresay and not sufficiently
substantiated.

Defendant further states that the Court committed
additional error by allowing the admission into evidence of
State's exhibits 10, 13, and 14, all of which had no probative
value and were inflammatory and prejudicial to the Defendant.

Defendant further states the Court committed error
in failing to charge the jury on the element of anger as
there was evidence presented sufficient to entitle the jury to
consider this point.

> BROWN & HORN
>
> By_____
> James O. Brown
> Attorneys for Charles O. Forman

PROOF OF SERVICE

I hereby certify that a copy of the foregoing Motion
and Memorandum were personally delivered to the Franklin
County Prosecutor's Office on this 3rd day of May, 1971.

> _____
> James O. Brown

The case was then appealed and following are some of the pleadings that were filed.

FIGURE 9-7

```
         IN THE COURT OF COMMON PLEAS, FRANKLIN COUNTY, OHIO
                        CRIMINAL DIVISION

State of Ohio                       :

              Plaintiff             :

   vs.                              :      Case No. 35,000

Charles O. Forman                   :

              Defendant             :


                    MOTION PERTAINING TO BILL OF
                 EXCEPTIONS, COSTS, AND APPOINTMENT OF
                               COUNSEL
        _____

          Now comes the Defendant, Charles O. Forman, by his
     attorney and moves that the Court order the costs of the
     Bill of Exceptions and all other appeal costs be taxed
     as other costs herein.

          The Defendant further moves the Court order a
     transcript of the Defendant's trial be produced at the
     State's expense and that James O. Brown be appointed to
     represent him in the instant action.  The Defendant is
     indigent and unable to pay said costs.

          The Defendant further moves the Court for an order
     extending the time of the filing of said Bill of Exceptions
     to August 2, 1971.

                              BROWN & HORN

                              By_____
                              James O. Brown
                              Attorneys for Defendant
                              330 Main Street
                              Any Town, U. S. A.
```

FIGURE 9-7a

IN THE COURT OF COMMON PLEAS, FRANKLIN COUNTY,
OHIO CRIMINAL DIVISION

State of Ohio   :

          Plaintiff   :

vs.   :   Case No.
                                         35,000

Charles O. Forman   :

          Defendant   :

ENTRY

This day this cause came on to be heard and for good cause shown, it is the finding and the order of this Court that the cost of the Bill of Exceptions and all other appeal costs be taxed as other costs herein.

It is further ordered that a transcript of the Defendant's trial be produced at State's expense, and that Attorney James O. Brown be appointed to represent the Defendant in the instant action. The Court finds that the Defendant is indigent and unable to pay said costs.

It is further ordered that the time to file the Bill of Exceptions is extended to August 3, 19_____.

                                  _____
                                        JUDGE

Approved:

_____
Prosecuting Attorney
Attorney for Plaintiff-Appellee

_____
James O. Brown
Attorney for Defendant-Appellant

FIGURE 9-8

IN THE COURT OF COMMON PLEAS, FRANKLIN COUNTY, OHIO CRIMINAL DIVISION

State of Ohio   :

               Plaintiff   :

     vs.   :   Case No.
                                               35,000

Charles O. Forman   :

              Defendant   :

PRECIPE

TO THE CLERK:

Please prepare and file in the Court of Appeals for Franklin County, Ohio, the transcript of the docket and journal entries and all original papers in the above-entitled action.

Please assist in securing from Messrs. Strong and Hill, Court Reporters, the Bill of Exceptions, transcript of the trial on the above-noted case which commenced on April 26, 19_____, and filing in the trial court promptly to conform with the Court rules.

                              BROWN & HORN

                              By_____
                              James O. Brown
                              Attorney for Defendant-Appellant

FIGURE 9-9

IN THE COURT OF COMMON PLEAS, FRANKLIN COUNTY, OHIO

CRIMINAL DIVISION

State of Ohio   :

    Plaintiff   :

vs.   : Case No. 35,000

Charles O. Forman   :

    Defendant :

NOTICE OF APPEAL

Now comes the Defendant, Charles O. Forman, by his attorney and gives Notice of Appeal to the Court of Appeals of Franklin County from the Order and Entry of the Court of Common Pleas of Franklin County entered on the 24th day of May, 1971. Said Appeal is on Questions of Law.

       BROWN & HORN

       By_____
       James O. Brown
       Attorney for Defendant-Appellant
       330 Main Street
       Any Town, U. S. A.
       Phone: 223-2241

CERTIFICATE OF SERVICE

I certify that a copy of the foregoing Notice of Appeal was delivered to the Franklin County Prosecutor's Office on the 21st day of June, 1971, by counsel for the Defendant.

       BROWN & HORN

       By_____
       James O. Brown
       Attorney for Defendant

FIGURE 9-10

IN THE COURT OF APPEALS OF FRANKLIN COUNTY, OHIO

State of Ohio   :

      Plaintiff-Appellee   :

vs.   :   Case No. 15,000

Charles O. Forman   :

      Defendant-Appellant   :

MOTION TO SET TIME FOR FILING
ASSIGNMENT OF ERROR

Now comes the Defendant, Charles O. Forman, by his
attorney, having duly filed his Notice of Appeal to the
order of the Court of Common Pleas, on May 27, 1971, pursuant
to Sections 2953.04, et seq., Revised Code, having filed
a praecipe with the Clerk to forward the transcript of
the original papers, and having requested a Bill of
Exceptions be prepared, authenticated, and filed with this
Court within the time limits prescribed by the Court of
Common Pleas, and requests this Court of Appeals to extend
rule day for the filing of Assignments of Error and Brief
thirty (30) days after the filing of the Bill of Exceptions
in the Court of Appeals.

                    BROWN & HORN

                    By_____
                    James O. Brown
                    Attorney for Defendant-Appellant

CERTICIATE OF SERVICE

I hereby certify a copy of the foregoing Motion was
delivered to the Franklin County Prosecutor's Office on the
____day of June, 1971.

                    BROWN & HORN

                    By_____
                    James O. Brown
                    Attorney for Defendant-Appellant

FIGURE 9-11

IN THE COURT OF APPEALS OF FRANKLIN COUNTY, OHIO

State of Ohio	:	
Plaintiff-Appellee	:	
vs.	:	Case No.
		15,000
Charles O. Forman	:	
Defendant-Appellant		

Entry Setting Time for
Filing Assignment of Error

It appearing to the Court that the Defendant, Charles O. Forman, having duly filed his Notice of Appeal to the order of the Court of Common Pleas, dated May 27, 19_____, pursuant to Sections 2953.04, *et seq.,* Revised Code of Ohio, and filed a praecipe with the Clerk to forward the transcript of the original papers, and having requested a Bill of Exceptions be prepared, authenticated, and filed with this Court within the time limits prescribed by the Court of Common Pleas, it is the order of this Court that rule day for the filing of Assignments of Error and Brief is to be set thirty (30) days after the filing of the Bill of exceptions in this Court.

—————————————————
JUDGE

Approved:

—————————————————
Franklin County Prosecutor
Attorney for Plaintiff-Appellee

—————————————————
James O. Brown
Attorney for Defendant-Appellant

Sometimes it is necessary to file a "Motion to Suppress." The following sample was taken from an actual case (fictitious name) wherein a young college girl set fire to the dormitory in which she was living and wherein another coed died.

FIGURE 9-12

IN THE COURT OF COMMON PLEAS, FRANKLIN COUNTY, OHIO

State of Ohio   :

                          Plaintiff   :   Case No.
                                                                    36,000

        vs.   :

Harriet Cordella   :

                          Defendant   :

Motion to Suppress

Now comes the defendant, Harriet Cordella, by and through her counsel, and respectfully moves this Court for an order suppressing as evidence in this case all or any items taken from the dormitory room of HARRIET CORDELLA, during May 20, 19———, and June 1, 19———, while she was a resident student in Lincoln Tower, of Ohio State University; and

For an order suppressing as evidence in this case, all statements, oral, written, electronic, taped, stenographic or otherwise, alleged to have been made by the defendant, in regard to a fire occurring in an Ohio State University Dormitory, Lincoln Tower, on or about May 22, 19———, which fire is the subject matter of an indictment charging this defendant in said indictment, number 36,000, with the alleged violation of Ohio Revised Code Section 2901.06, Manslaughter First Degree, and Ohio Revised Code Section 2907.02, Arson, for the following reasons:

1. The taking of various items and property from the defendant's dormitory room was an illegal taking.

2. Any and all such statements alleged to have been taken or given by this defendant were involuntary.

3. The foregoing actions constitute a violation of defendant's Constitutional rights as guaranteed her under the Ohio Constitution by virtue of Article I, Sections 1-10-14; and the United States Constitution as guaranteed her under the Fourth, Fifth, Sixth and Fourteenth Amendments of said Constitution.

4. The failure of the Court to grant defendant's motion will in effect deny her the right to a fair and impartial trial.

WHEREFORE, defendant prays that all items taken from her dormitory room on or about the above stated dates be suppressed and that all statements alleged to have been given by this defendant in whatever manner be suppressed.

> BROWN & HORN
> Attorneys for the Defendant
> 330 Main Street
> Anytown, U.S.A.
> 223-2241
>
> By:_____
> James O. Brown

Of course each criminal proceeding is different, but you can make up sample pleadings for your form book that might be repeated.

Pointers to Witnesses

Your attorney may wish you to prepare a set of instructions to witnesses which he may wish to have duplicated and kept on hand to hand any witnesses he may be calling to testify for his client. The "Pointers to Witnesses" shown in Chapter Seven are applicable to all types of trial cases as well as domestic cases.

You and Tax Law

What can you do to expedite the filling out of income tax returns? How much of the work can you shoulder, leaving the attorney to work more with income tax law and less with the accounting end?

Typing and Verifying the Lawyer's Figures

You can do much to insure the preparation of arithmetic-error-free returns. There are two types of errors to guard against: the attorney's errors in calculation and your typing errors. A good time-saver in the typing of the return to avoid so much retyping in case an error is detected later is to type the return backwards!

For example, suppose a return consists of the 1040, Schedules B, C, and D, and perhaps a few tables or explanations of certain lines on Schedule C. Put your work sheets in order first. That is, start with the 1040, add Schedule B on top, Schedule C and the accompanying explanations and then Schedule D. When you start typing, type Schedule D first, double-check it on your adding machine for errors, check to see if the figures are carried over properly to the 1040, and then go on to the explanations of Schedule C. After you have typed the explanations, check them on the adding machine, check the totals to see that they are carried forward correctly to Schedule C. Then type Schedule C, proceed in the same manner, always checking each schedule against the 1040 for carry-over figures.

By the time you are ready to type the 1040 itself, you have an accurate return up to that point. Or, if you have found an error in the attorney's computation, any correction can be made to the 1040 before you type it. After typing the 1040, double-check the addition and subtraction on the adding machine, using the tax tables to compute the tax, and you have a finished error-free return. Always double-check the Social Security number for errors as it is important that the client be identified by his proper number. If Internal Revenue Service finds that the Social Security number is incorrect, they will delay the processing of the return.

When you double-check the attorney's computation on the adding machine, you will also catch typing errors. This method of typing applies to any type of return—individual, corporation, partnership, fiduciary—and of course, the tax bracket wouldn't make any difference, whether the income is under $10,000 or over.

Actual application of the tax laws would, of course, have to be done by the attorney-preparer, who spends time and care keeping up-to-date on all changes in the law, usually by a tax service such as Prentice-Hall's Tax Guide.

Billing the Clients

Billing the clients is a necessity and should be done as soon as the return is typed. The attorney no doubt has set a fee for each client based on complexity of the tax return and to speed up the process of billing you may bill each client the same amount as he or she was billed the previous year. To make the billing easier, make a notation on the file copy of the tax return. The following year the billing can be done with that figure.

In typing out the statement, list each schedule prepared for the client. This will give him some idea of the amount of work involved and exactly what he is being billed for. The billing should read as follows:

> Tax Service as follows:
>   Form 1040
>   Schedule B
>   Schedule C
>   Schedule D
>   Supporting Schedules
>   City return
>   County return $75.00

If your office maintains a ledger card for each client for billing purposes, post the billing to the ledger card and note it on the current copy of the tax return in the file. ,

In some isolated cases there will be additional work for a client that wasn't done the year before. For example, he might have sold and bought a residence and the attorney might have had to make up a Form 2119, which he didn't prepare that year. This might change the amount of the billing, and it is wise for you to watch for this situation and check with the attorney to see if he wishes to increase the amount of the fee. Likewise, watch for the opposite situation, in which the attorney does less work than the year before, and check with the attorney to see if he wishes to decrease the fee in all fairness to the client.

Getting the Return to the Client

If the law office maintains a good copier machine, ignore the carbon paper in typing tax returns. A much easier method is to type one copy of the return (errors can be corrected more easily, quickly and neatly without carbon), then make two copies on the copier, one to be sent to the client and one to be retained by the attorney. If the completed tax return is put in the proper order before the copies are made it will come out in proper order and save assembly time.

When the copies are assembled it is well to use a rubber stamp marked "Client's Copy" on the copy going to the client since many clients cannot discern the original from the copy. Then attach the W-2 forms to the original 1040 (Copy B) in the place designated by Internal Revenue Service (they change the position from time to time).

Address a large manila envelope to the client and prepare an instruction sheet. The instruction sheet may be typed up and run off on the copier. The instructions should tell each client exactly what returns he is getting, how he should sign them, and how much he should pay, if anything.

Enclose with the return one of IRS's preaddressed envelopes for the client's convenience in mailing his return to IRS after typing the client's name and address in the upper left-hand corner.

Instructions

	Tax Due	Refund	Due Date	Signed by Husband & Wife
( ) U.S. Individual Income	$_____	$_____	Apr. 15, 19____	_____
( ) U.S. Estimated Tax	$_____	_____	Apr. 15, 19____ Voucher 1	_____
( ) City Tax	$_____	_____	_____	_____
( ) City Estimate	$_____	_____	_____	_____
( ) County Tax Entire Year ____ 1/2 ____	$_____	_____	_____	_____

( ) County return has been put on our extension list and is not due until _____ It will be mailed to you about _____

Special Instructions

Please mail the returns in the envelopes provided by the due date, after signing and enclosing checks, if required. Checks for U.S. tax should be payable to Internal Revenue Service and you should put your Social Security number on the face of the check. Checks for city tax should be made payable to Treasurer, City of _____ Checks for county tax should be made payable to _____ County Treasurer.

If we have enclosed a Federal estimate you should make payment No. 1 by April 15, and the other three payments should be made as follows:

Voucher No. 2 - by June 15
Voucher No. 3 - by September 15
Voucher No. 4 - by January 15 of next year

If we have enclosed City estimates, the same procedure should be used as for the Federal.

If you have any questions, please call

Homer J. Black
BLACK & JONES

FIGURE 10-1

As of this writing IRS is requiring that the preaddressed labels they send out with the form booklet be transferred to each return.

Place the return, the client's copy, the billing, the envelope to IRS, and the instruction sheet in the large manila envelope addressed to the client, after the attorney has signed the return as preparer; seal it, weigh it for postage, and mail it in sufficient time to reach the client before the April 15 deadline.

It is helpful if you note the date of mailing on the office copy as a matter of check-up if the client calls and inquires about his return.

Clients who have large, complicated returns may wish to come to the office to pick up their returns.

When the Lawyer Uses Computer Service

There are several good computer services available for processing tax returns. While the primary saving is in your time, the lawyer may save considerable time also. The lawyer may, with computer service, interview the client, fill out the interview sheet, and stop there. The computer will compute the tax and print out the required number of copies of the return.

However, for the tax lawyer who wishes to do his own computing, the computer service furnishes a summary sheet, and the computer verifies all computations. If it finds an error, it corrects it. If your lawyer uses a computer, while you are relieved of typing the returns and verifying figures, there are other duties you can perform. First, you can serve as a traffic manager. As the interview sheets are completed you can prepare them for mailing to the computer center. This usually involves typing out a transmittal form with the names of the clients being sent in for processing. It may involve using a rubber stamp with the preparer's name on it and placing it on the required place on the interview sheet (preprinted labels are sent after the first year), or placing the firm's label carrying the number assigned to the account by the computer service on the interview sheet.

When the acknowledgement copy of the transmittal form is returned, it will carry a projected shipping date. Refer to this in case a client inquires about the status of his return. Keep the acknowledgement copies and the copies of the transmittal forms together until the return has arrived, along with the final transmittal copy.

FIGURE 10-2

3800-52   002 CC

Form **1040** US Department of the Treasury / Internal Revenue Service
Individual Income Tax Return 🌐 19__

For the year January 1–December 31, 1970, or other taxable year beginning................................ 1970, ending.......................... 19...........

First name and initial (if joint return, use first names and middle initials of both)	Last name	Your social security number
JOHN W AND SHIRLEY	LEONARD	523 12 2741
Present home address (Number and street or rural route)		Spouse's social security number
1533 CLARION ROAD		465 14 9003
City, town or post office, State and ZIP code	Occu-pation	Yours RETAILER
MIAMI FLORIDA 33133		Spouse's HOUSEWIFE

Filing Status—check only one:

1 ☐ Single; 2 ☒ Married filing jointly (even if only one had income)

3 ☐ Married filing separately and spouse is also filing. If this item checked give spouse's social security number in space above and enter first name here ►

4 ☐ Unmarried Head of Household

5 ☐ Surviving widow(er) with dependent child

6 ☐ Married filing separately and spouse is not filing

Exemptions Regular / 65 or over / Blind Enter number of boxes checked ►

7 Yourself . . . . ☒ ☐ ☐

8 Spouse (applies only if item 2 or 6 is checked) ☒ ☒ ☐

9 First names of your dependent children who lived with you . . . . Enter number ► 1

10 Number of other dependents (from line 34) . . . . ►

11 Total exemptions claimed . . . . ► 4

Income

12 Wages, salaries, tips, etc. (Attach Forms W–2 to back.)		12	
13a Dividends (see pages 5 and 9 of instr.) $ 360 13b Less exclusion $ 185 Balance ►		13c	175
(Also list in Part I of Schedule B, if gross dividends and other distributions are over $100)			
14 Interest. Enter total here (also list in Part II of Schedule B, if total is over $100)		14	5,199
15 Income other than wages, dividends, and interest (from line 40)		15	18,760
16 Total (add lines 12, 13c, 14 and 15)		16	24,134
17 Adjustments to income (such as "sick pay," moving expense, etc. from line 45)		17	
18 Adjusted gross income (subtract line 17 from line 16)		18	24,134

● See page 2 of instructions for rules under which the IRS will figure your tax and surcharge.
● If you do not itemize deductions and line 18 is under $10,000, find tax in Tables. Enter tax on line 19.
● If you itemize deductions or line 18 is $10,000 or more, go to line 46 to figure tax.

Tax and Surcharge

19 Tax (Check if from: Tax Tables 1–15 ☐ Tax Rate Schedule X, Y, or Z ☐ Schedule D ☒ or Schedule G ☐)		19	3,905
20 Tax surcharge. See Tax Surcharge Tables A, B and C in instructions. (If you claim retirement income credit, use Schedule R to figure surcharge.)		20	94
21 Total (add lines 19 and 20)		21	3,999

Payments and Credits

22 Total credits (from line 55)		22	136
23 Income tax (subtract line 22 from line 21)		23	3,863
24 Other taxes (from line 61)		24	538
25 Total (add lines 23 and 24)		25	4,401
26 Total Federal income tax withheld (attach Forms W–2 to back). 26			Make check or money order payable to Internal Revenue Service.
27 1970 Estimated tax payments (include 1969 overpayment allowed as a credit) 27 5,000			
28 Other payments (from line 65) 28			
29 Total (add lines 26, 27, and 28)		29	5,000

Bal. Due or Refund

30 If line 25 is larger than line 29, enter BALANCE DUE. Pay in full with return . . . . . ►		30	
31 If line 29 is larger than line 25, enter OVERPAYMENT . . . . ►		31	599
32 Line 31 to be: (a) Credited on 1971 estimated tax ► $ 599; (b) Refunded ► $			

Under penalties of perjury, I declare that I have examined this return, including accompanying schedules and statements, and to the best of my knowledge and belief it is true, correct, and complete.

Sign here

Your signature _____ Date _____

Signature of preparer other than taxpayer, based on all information of which he has any knowledge. Date _____
WRIGHT AND BUTLER
MIAMI, FLORIDA

Spouse's signature (if filing jointly, BOTH must sign even if only one had income)   Address

FIGURE 10-3

BATCH NO.	DATE RECEIVED	PROJECTED SHIPPING DATE	RETURNS

ABOVE FOR COMPUTAX USE ONLY

CC COMPUTAX ®   **TRANSMITTAL FORM**

IF YOU WISH TO SPECIFY A METHOD OF DELIVERY OTHER THAN COMPUTAX'S CHOICE - CHECK BELOW.

REGULAR MAIL ☐   AIR MAIL ☐   UPS ☐

IMPORTANT: When requesting a state return for a state other than that in which your firm is located, PLEASE use a separate transmittal for that state and indicate the state in the box to the right.

STATE RETURNS FOR

CLIENT'S NAME	UNIT NO.	COMPUTAX USE ONLY

CUSTOMER'S COPY

Then staple all the copies together and place them in a file for checking with the billing.

When the printed-out returns come in from the computer center, quickly check the attorney's computation on the summary sheet as to the amount of tax due or to be refunded with the printed-out return. If they agree, the return is ready to be mailed to the client. If there is a discrepancy, the return should go to the attorney to see where the error is and if the attorney made the error, the return can go to the client.

The computer does not make errors in computation. Any errors by the computer result from the wrong information being fed into it, and the persons who feed the cards can, of course, make errors. However, all computerized returns are verified by several different persons, so chances of error on the computer's part are minimal.

Errors on printed-out returns may also result from the preparer making a wrong entry on the interview sheet.

THE DIAGNOSTIC SHEET

With each printed-out return comes a diagnostic sheet which pinpoints any discrepancies in the return and explains any changes made in the preparer's figures. Check the diagnostic sheet before

FIGURE 10-4

PHILLIP E AND EILEEN W SHARPE		6631-53		028
COMPUTAX DIAGNOSTIC REPORT - 19__				PAGE 1
COMMENTS		SUBMITTED	COMPUTED	DIFFER.

GUIDELINE EXCEEDS GENERAL SALES TAX				
JT DATA-SPOUSE SOC SEC NO. MISSING				
INCOME AVERAGING DATA IS PRESENT				
INC AVG USED-TAX SAVING OF	FED	10,474	10,150	324
AVG BASE PERIOD INC FOR 19__-19__	FED		24,200	
INCOME NEEDED IN 19__ FOR AVERAGING	FED		35,689	
FOREIGN TAX CREDIT ELECTION BLANK				
ASSUMED OVERALL LIMITATION				
SCH C INC ASSUMED TAXPAYERS FOR SE				

giving it to the preparer, as there may be an error that you can correct, such as a missing social security number, a missing filing status, a missing occupation, etc. Take care of this type of error yourself by filling in the missing information on the return and all copies.

VERIFYING THE INVOICE FROM THE COMPUTER CENTER

When the invoice arrives from the computer center, it will list each return processed by name of client, the charges per return, and any other charges made (such as charges for pro formas). Note: Pro formas are interview sheets with all of the reusable information preprinted the following year. They are furnished after the first year and save considerable writing out of material that is repetitious. Take your transmittal copies received back with the printed-out returns and check off each name on the invoice to make certain it was actually processed. The billings will come periodically. The diagnostic sheet will also show the amount charged for each return with a detailed listing of each charge made. The attorney may wish to use the charges on the diagnostic sheet to compute his own fee to the client, adding the charges for his time and services to that of the computer charges.

Computer charges per return may run slightly higher than if typed by you, but the savings in your time and the attorney's time more than offset the slight additional expense.

BILLING AND GETTING THE COMPUTERIZED RETURNS TO THE CLIENTS

The billing procedure and the sending of the returns to the clients can be done exactly the same as for typed returns as explained earlier. The W-2's must be attached to the computerized returns as they are not sent in to the computer center.

Following are names and addresses of computer services for Income Tax returns:

Computax Corp. (Commerce Clearing House)
910 N. Sepulveda Boulevard
El Segundo, California 90245

Autotax
Fallschurch, Virginia 22000

Digitax
Greenvale, N.Y. 11548

Filing the Tax Returns

Handling of the filing of income tax returns is no problem if each client has his own folder which is separate from any other matters. Maintain a special income tax file with the clients' folders filed alphabetically. The attorney's work sheets can be retained as file copies from year to year so that the attorney has a complete record of his client's tax history.

Making Appointments for Tax Clients

If the attorney has built up a good practice for income tax returns, making appointments and handling clients when they come into the office must be done methodically. Often the attorney will build up an income tax practice as a business-getter. A client who comes in at first just to get a tax return made out may later have an estate to be settled, or become involved in an accident and file a personal injury suit, or buy or sell a home, but you can make appointments for tax returns as the calls come in. Check with your attorney to find out about how long he needs to make out the average return (or fill in an interview sheet if he uses computer), and then judge how close together the appointments can be made. When the client arrives in the office you can pull his file and hand it to the attorney when you take the client into his office.

Processing tax returns can be enjoyable if done in an efficient, business-like manner.

You as a Legal Assistant

There is a movement afoot to train the legal secretary to be more than a secretary, to go beyond tasks that require primarily the exercise of functional skills, or even beyond tasks requiring the exercise of care and moderate originality, to tasks requiring an analytical skill and intellectual judgment. Sometimes the new position is known as "Legal Assistant," "Legal Technician," or "Paralegal Aide."

Whatever name is applied, there is one thing that evolves out of the movement. You, as the legal secretary of the future who wishes to assume the new role, will have to have more education than the average legal secretary of today, who stopped with a high school diploma.

The first school of its type to offer such a course piloted its first class in October of 1970 at the Institute for Paralegal Training in Philadelphia. The 14-week course, at a cost of $500, offers the graduate a choice of one of five different areas: real estate, corporate law, wills and estates, litigation, and general law practice. Graduates command more salary than a legal secretary, but less than a law student. They earn about $8,000 per year.

The University of Utah College of Law has piloted a training course for the Legal Assistant. The program was approved by the American Bar Association in February 1971, and is eminently successful. The course of study is known as a "system," and systems have been completed in the areas of probate, corporation, and divorce.

The pioneers of the program recognized that the only tasks or procedures in the practice of law with respect to which the utilization of a lay assistant could practically be applied are those which are repetitive. In other words, a lay assistant can only be usefully employed in those tasks which can be routinized so that standard forms may be used and standardized procedures may be implemented. If the task or procedure is novel, it is almost universally within the deliberative province of a lawyer by its very nature. Thus, the first time a lawyer is confronted with the filing of a petition in probate, he should develop his own form and procedure. But after he has performed this function half a dozen times or so—that is, when he has routinized the procedure—he ought to have developed a system which you can follow under his supervision. The developers of the program also recognized that experience indicates that a great deal of each lawyer's time may be tied up in tasks of a more or less routine nature, the degree of uniformity depending upon the nature of the practice. For example, a lawyer with a probate specialty could conceivably spend his entire time dictating the complete contents of each probate he handles throughout his professional career; whereas, perhaps 85% of these "legal" functions could be performed by a trained lay specialist. Similarly, each other specialty in the law develops its own routine tasks. Even so highly a customized practice as litigation, when properly analyzed and systematized, can be highly routinized with commensurately high utilization of lay assistants.

The "Systems" approach is divided into two branches, (1) the administrative or "business" branch, and (2) the substantive or professional branch. Included among administrative procedures are: time keeping, accounting, personnel management, investigation, filing, library, reception duties, and the like. Included in the substantive branch are all of the substantive law divisions such as real estate, securities, bankruptcy, civil litigation, and the like.

Requirement for registration for the course is a bachelor's degree or the equivalent.

The School feels that a national association should be formed to establish standards and quality control procedures to insure compatibility and reciprocity of programs and competency of System graduates. It suggests that the leadership of such a phase might be assumed by the American Bar Association.

Thus, you as the legal secretary of tomorrow, as the legal assistant, are faced with a challenge to extend your usefulness into vast new areas of endeavor.

Bibliography

ONE

Definitions of Code Napoleon and Roman Law reprinted from *Black's Law Dictionary*, Fourth Edition, by permission of West Publishing Co., St. Paul, Minn., owner of copyright.

Canons of the American Bar Association reprinted by permission of The American Bar Association.

TWO

Sections on arrangement of the law library from *Manual of Procedures for Private Law Libraries*, by Elizabeth Finley, rev. ed. Rothman, 1966, published by the American Association of Law Libraries, copyright owner.

THREE

"Handling the Incoming Mail" adapted from the author's article, "The Daily Mail," reprinted from *From Nine to Five* by permission of The Dartnell Corporation, Chicago, Illinois.

"Being a Personal Secretary" adapted from author's article "Being a Personal Secretary," reprinted from *Modern Secretary* by permission of Allied Publications, Inc., Fort Lauderdale, Florida.

FOUR

"Ordering Supplies" adapted from author's article "To Be in Good Supply," reprinted from *Today's Secretary*, Gregg-McGraw-Hill Publication, New York, N.Y.

"Supervising the Junior Secretary" adapted from the author's article, "How to Help Employees Do a Better Job," reprinted from *The Woman Supervisor*, The Dartnell Corporation, Chicago, Illinois.

"Frankness in Talking over Problems Between the Lawyer and the Secretary" adapted from author's article "Are You and Your Boss Compatible?," reprinted from *Modern Secretary* by permission of Allied Publications, Inc., Fort Lauderdale, Florida.

FIVE

"The Alphabetical File" filing tips reprinted from "File to Find" by permission of Oxford Pendaflex Corporation, Garden City, New York.

TEN

"Typing and Verifying the Lawyer's Figures" adapted from author's article "Preparing Clients' Income Tax Returns," reprinted with permission from *L.S. for Legal Secretaries,* published by the Bureau of Business Practice, 24 Rope Ferry Road, Waterford, Conn., Copyright 1965.

Sample forms for computer service reproduced by permission of Computax Corporation, El Segundo, California.

CONCLUSION

Description of the "Systems" approach of the University of Utah College of Law for Legal Assistants used with permission of Kline D. Strong of the staff of the University of Utah College of Law.

Index